Potatoes

Bodo A. Schieren

Potatoes

D

Dealerfield

Published in Germany in 1989 by Südwest Verlag GmbH & Co. KG, Munich
This edition first published in the United Kingdom in 1994 by Transedition Books, a division of
Andromeda Oxford Limited, 11-15 The Vineyard, Abingdon, Oxon OX14 3PX, England

Photography: Bodo A. Schieren
Recipes and food arrangement: Jürgen Suré
Translation: Isabel Varea in association with First Edition Translations Ltd, Cambridge

Printed in 1994 in Spain

This edition specially printed for Dealerfield Ltd, 1994

ISBN 1 85927 015 8

Contents

Foreword

*T*he potato, which is native to South America, has, along with bread, become one of our staple foods. Many of us cherish childhood memories of the joys of munching chips and crisps or tucking into mashed or jacket potatoes. As adults, we appreciate not only the tasty snacks potatoes offer, but also the nutritional value they provide to our diet.

To the cook, the potato offers a challenge, calling for imagination and ingenuity. The humble spud is not there simply to soak up the gravy. It can be prepared in all kinds of simple and sophisticated ways, to be served hot or cold, as an accompaniment or main course, with only the simplest seasonings or with such gourmet ingredients as salmon or caviare.

Potatoes *begins with the history of the potato, and describes how it is grown and harvested. It provides information about calorie content and nutritional values, about herbs and spices, and about what to look for when buying potatoes and how to store them. Above all, the clearly explained recipes are designed to encourage you to experience for yourself just how refined and versatile potatoes can be. The book's elegant presentation and fascinating and informative text promise not only a feast for the eyes, but also culinary delights of the highest order.*

Potato

Danish Kartoffel

Dutch aardappel

Finnish peruna

French pomme de terre

German Kartoffel

Greek γεω,υηλον

Hungarian burgonys, pityóka, kolompír, krumpli

Italian patata

Latin Solanum tuberosum

Norwegian Potet, Potetes

Portuguese batata

Spanish patata

Swedish jordpäron, potates

Drawings by Poma de Ayala,
from the book Los Mezes i Años,
1584–1614

Introducing the Potato

The potato is an unassuming vegetable. Unlike many others, it does not catch the eye with its bright colour or strong flavour. You can buy it anywhere, and it is easy to cook. Indeed, it is one of the mainstays of our diet. However, this tuber is a homely deity, to whom human understanding has assigned a variety of roles during its long life. The potato has been seen as a god of nature and the work of the devil, a miracle cure and the height of depravity, a means of survival and an aphrodisiac. For years, potatoes were thought to be fattening, and many people refused to eat them. Today, however, they have finally taken on a new, glittering image as a healthy, low-calorie and palatable source of energy.

The tempestuous career of the potato began in the heights of the Andes, in Peru, Bolivia, Ecuador and Chile. According to evidence found among 8,000-year-old Peruvian burial objects, potatoes have been cultivated in this part of the world since the dawn of time. Maize and potatoes were the staple diet of the earliest inhabitants of the Andean region. Potatoes, however, can be cultivated at up to 3,000 metres (10,000 ft) above sea-level, where maize will no longer grow. Well before the time of the Incas, the ancient Quechua Indians not only consumed potatoes, they also worshipped them. To them, Nature was a divine force and the potato was a life-giving goddess who had to be appeased to keep her in a benevolent mood. We know that the Incas also revered the potato because they made potato-shaped jugs and other cult objects to place in the tombs of the dead.

Before the Europeans set out to colonize America and the rest of the world, the vast Inca nation was considered invincible by surrounding peoples. The Incas were experts in making provision for times of famine. It was they who invented freeze-dried potatoes. The Incas would leave the potatoes out in the open to freeze in the chill night air. They were then thawed in the daytime under the blazing sun, and left until they dried out, all the water content having been extracted in a completely natural way. After that, they would keep indefinitely. These edible 'stones' could be soaked at any time to make them soft again, and then they could be eaten.

When they discovered the Americas, the Spanish conquistadores were more than a little surprised by these stone-hard tubers. They were first reported by Pedro de Cieza de León, a member of a Spanish expedition to the high Andes in 1538:

It is very cold there, no maize grows, neither are there any trees. Papas are the mainstay of the inhabitants. They dry them in the sun and store them from one

10

From left to right: Sowing seed potatoes, Weeding the field, Harvest, Filling the potato store

harvest to the next. They are then called chuño. *When boiled, they become as tender as chestnuts. Their skin is no thicker than a truffle's.*

Supposedly in the same year, de León's comrade-in-arms, Juan de Castellanos, noted that in the village of Sorocata in the River Magdalena region (now Colombia) there were 'maize, beans and truffles'. He found that the so-called 'truffles' were very good to eat. He wrote: 'They have floury roots, and a good flavour. They are a valuable asset to the Indians and a delicious food, even for Spaniards.'

It was not long before the conquistadores were bringing potatoes back to Spain as souvenirs. One of the first recorded offerings of potatoes was presented by a loyal subject to King Philip II in 1565. The gift package may well have included a list of the healing properties attributed to potatoes by the Indians: they laid raw potato on broken bones, rubbed the forehead with raw potato to relieve headaches, carried a potato in the pocket to ward off rheumatism, and ate potatoes to cure indigestion. In any case, Philip sent the newly discovered vegetable to Pope Pius V, in the hope of improving the papal state of health. The benevolent pontiff gave a few tubers to an ailing cardinal in the Netherlands, who then shared his present with the Prefect of Mons. The latter seems to have planted his potatoes in his garden in order to pass some samples on to the then-famous botanist Charles d'Ecluse, who, following the current fashion for Latinized names, called himself Carolus Clusius. In 1573 Clusius became gardens superintendent to the Holy Roman Emperor Rudolph II and was also responsible for the various pleasure parks of Count Wilhelm IV of Hesse. To please his illustrious employers, Clusius embellished their borders with the rare potato plants, with their sweetly perfumed pink, blue and mauve blossoms. Proudly, the Emperor and Count sent cuttings to their friends and relations. Count Wilhelm wrote to Christian I, Prince-Elector of Saxony:

We are sending Your Highness a plant, which we obtained from Italy a few years ago and which is called taratouphli. *This plant grows in the ground and has pretty flowers, a pleasant odour and, underneath, roots from which many* tubera *hang; these, when boiled, are good to eat. They must first be boiled in water, until the outer skin comes off, then the water must be poured away and the potato finally seethed in butter until done.*

11

So people knew that the potato was edible. None the less, around the turn of the seventeenth century it was grown chiefly as an exotic ornamental or medicinal plant in the parks of spiritual and temporal rulers. It also flourished in the herb gardens of medical schools and universities, and probably in the kitchen gardens of monastic communities or wealthy aristocratic families. In botanical catalogues the potato appeared under garden and healing plants.

It was highly prized by doctors, botanists and princes, not least because they believed it to have certain mysterious powers, discreetly claiming that it 'enhances the conjugal function'. Potato recipes were tried out in the kitchens of many noble houses, but with not much success. With its delicate, bland taste, it could not compete with the flavours of the many spices and other delicacies that were by this time emerging from every corner of the world. Only later would large-scale potato cultivation begin in Europe.

It started in Spain. Accounts kept at the hospital in Seville reveal that from 1573 onwards locally grown potatoes were regularly delivered to the kitchens. The crews of the many ships heading for the South American colonies had long been accustomed to feeding on potatoes. The Spaniards had quickly learned to provision their ships with the Incas' crops. On ships where potatoes were on the menu, a fortunate side-effect was that the crews escaped the ravages of scurvy, a disease dreaded by every seafarer.

Potatoes also found their way to the British Isles. English history books have long credited the much-admired Sir Francis Drake, famed for his circumnavigation of the globe, with the introduction of potatoes to Britain. Historians always refer to a banquet on 4 April 1581 at which Drake served Queen Elizabeth I with potatoes brought back from his round-the-world voyage. However, the menu card, which still survives, shows that the feast included *batatas*, which was the name given to sweet potatoes in the West Indies at that time.

The 'real' potatoes were, in fact, in the luggage of Thomas Heriot, a British geographer. After a journey of exploration to Virginia, the first English colony in North America, Heriot returned home in 1586 on one of Drake's ships. Drake had captured some Spanish galleons in the Caribbean. In order to inspect the spoils and reload, he remained in dock at Cartagena for six weeks. It is most likely that Heriot met some of the local potato suppliers when they came aboard. The fact that Heriot was already carrying an assortment of plants from Virginia gave rise to the erroneous belief that the potato came from the same area, and that it was Drake who had discovered it. It appears in the great English book by John Gerard, *Herball or General History of Plants* as 'Potato of Virginia'. Since people like to believe in big names and enjoy good stories, Drake was accorded many literary tributes as the reputed discoverer of the potato.

However, although Drake did not discover it, he did indeed contribute to the spread of the potato. When his superior, Sir Walter Ralegh, retired to his estates in Ireland, Drake is said to have sent him a sack of seed potatoes. This sack may well have laid the foundation for the staple crop that was to feed the Irish people. Those not convinced by this story may prefer the following version: following the defeat of the Spanish Armada, many ships were wrecked off the coast of Ireland. Irish peasants who plundered the wrecks would have found potatoes on board and brought them ashore.

However it became established there, the potato's use as a food in Ireland helped to introduce it to Germany in this capacity. Although they were already thriving in the gardens of the German nobility, potatoes were not eaten by the ordinary people of Germany until the 'Glorious Revolution' of 1668, when German mercenaries fought in Ireland against the Stuart King James II, and were sustained mainly by Irish potatoes. Other mercenaries engaged in the War of the Spanish Succession tried growing potatoes in the Netherlands. Refugees fleeing to Germany from religious persecution in Spain and the Netherlands may have brought potatoes with them. German monasteries began to use potatoes to feed the poor. There is evidence that they were cultivated throughout Germany by the end of the seventeenth century.

Admittedly, the potato did not gain immediate universal acceptance in Europe. Further expansion was hindered by prejudice and superstition. The peasants had their own way of putting potatoes to the test: they threw them to their dogs. When the animals refused to eat them, it was assumed that they were not fit for human consumption. As the potato belongs to the same family as deadly nightshade, it was credited with diabolic powers. Some people said that potatoes contained narcotic substances, others claimed that they were poisonous, while still others believed that they caused such diseases as gout, anaemia, skin rashes and

rheumatism. Whatever information scholars may have had about this fruit of the earth simply did not get through to the rest of the population, particularly the rumour that frequent consumption of potatoes increased sexual urges to an extraordinary degree – a fact unlikely to safeguard the morals of the poor. It was only when the cereal crops failed in Germany between 1743 and 1755 that large numbers of farmers there were converted to the cause of potatoes. Frederick the Great commanded his subjects in the Eastern Provinces and Silesia to grow them, threatening any who refused with severe penalties. He needed well-fed, contented underlings, as well as strong, battle-ready soldiers for such conflicts as the Seven Years' War, in which the Prussian Army fought against the troops of Saxony, Austria, Russia, Sweden and France.

Right at the beginning of the war a Frenchman was taken prisoner by the Prussians. During his captivity the military apothecary Antoine Auguste Parmentier, then twenty years old, became acquainted with potatoes and later made them popular in his homeland. Until that time, the French had regarded the potato as a decorative motif. Whole dinner services painted with potato designs were ordered from porcelain manufacturers for pre-Revolutionary Versailles. Marie Antoinette's evening gowns were embroidered with potato flowers, and she used real blossoms to adorn her elaborate hairstyles. Meanwhile, Parmentier set out to promote the potato as an

alternative to bread, which was becoming ever more expensive. He was the winner of a competition, organized by the Academy of Science, to find ways to relieve hunger. However, he used trickery to encourage farmers to cultivate potatoes. In 1785 he convinced Louis XVI to allow him to plant a field of potatoes in the countryside near Paris. He then placed the field under military guard – but only in daylight hours. This made the peasants curious. These must be very valuable plants, they thought, and promptly stole them under cover of night.

Parmentier was a gourmet who created many potato recipes, the most famous of which are Potage Parmentier, an exquisite, thick potato soup, and Pommes Parmentier, diced potatoes fried with chives. Since Parmentier's day, the French have constantly invented sophisticated potato dishes. As a result, in France the potato never acquired the reputation it had elsewhere, as food for the poor. None the less, it gradually became accepted throughout Europe as an important part of subsistence diets, and by the beginning of the nineteenth century potatoes had become everyday fare for ordinary people.

There was a sudden outpouring of treatises on the potato, its cultivation and storage, its different varieties, as well as recipes for potato flour, dumplings, puddings and cakes, and instructions for the use of the vegetable in the production of glue, soap, beer and wine. There were even suggestions for recycling the leaves and skins for manufacturing paper. Particularly well-received were ideas for distilling potato spirit. This was a way of immediately preserving the highly perishable potato into a durable and easily saleable form.

There were two important effects of the increasingly widespread cultivation of the potato: a steep rise in population and a decline in the cultivation of other field crops. This ultimately had disastrous results. Repeated failures of the potato crop in the early 1840s led to famine in many parts of Central Europe. Ireland was the most notable example. After the potato began to be cultivated there late in the seventeenth century the population rose from about 5 million in 1800 to about 8 million in 1845, and the majority of these people were poor and lived on a diet mainly of potatoes. Potato production was not only intensive, but limited to one variety. When the fungal disease called blight infected one crop, it spread across the country like wildfire, resulting in the 'potato famines' of 1845, 1846 and 1848. Hundreds of thousands of people died. Of those who survived, hundreds of thousands more emigrated, most of them to North America. No doubt, the Irish were responsible for the spread of potatoes in the New World. In any case, the tuber that originated in South America soon became known as the 'Irish potato'.

The Industrial Revolution in the nineteenth century transformed potato cultivation in Europe.

Agricultural machines were developed, and the potato yield soared. This meant that fewer labourers were needed on the land, so workers flocked to the large towns and cities to find employment in factories. The new industrial working class needed food. With the introduction of railways, potatoes could quickly be transported to the centres of population. Everybody everywhere was now eating potatoes. Middle-class city dwellers, who at the beginning of the century had rejected potatoes as poor man's fare, came to relish the vegetable as much as country folk. Cooks everywhere were becoming more creative with potatoes. At the same time, growers could offer an ever-increasing range of potato varieties. At the great potato show in Germany in 1875 no less than 2,644 types were on show.

In each of the two world wars potatoes assumed a special importance in Europe. During the Second World War, for example, imports to Britain were severely restricted,and supplies of fresh produce, particularly vegetables, were limited. Because the potato plant is so prolific, millions of extra tonnes could be, and were, grown to keep the people fed in face of the other shortages. People relied heavily on the potato, and found a variety of imaginative ways in which to prepare them. When better times came and there was plenty of food for everybody, potatoes retained their popularity, particularly in the form of crisps and chips, the latter having been a popular part of the national diet

since the mid-nineteenth century. However, the obsession with slimming that began to sweep the world in the 1970s posed a threat to the traditional place of potatoes in diets everywhere: they were – and, by some people, still are – believed to be fattening. Fortunately for the sensational spud, as the trend towards healthy eating boomed in the 1980s the true worth of the potato was recognized: it contains far more vitamins and minerals and far fewer calories than was previously thought, and is a good source of dietary fibre.

If potato consumption had declined, it now enjoyed a renaissance. Top restaurant chefs and cookery writers led the way, creating ever more refined potato side-dishes, and even introducing potato-based main courses . Specialized potato restaurants sprang up in many cities, and street vendors selling hot baked potatoes with different toppings became a familiar sight. Manufacturers, who had already produced canned, powdered and frozen raw potatoes and potato products for the convenience of consumers, now introduced oven-ready and microwave chips so that this favourite food could be eaten even by people on low-fat diets. There is also, of course, a wide selection of different varieties of fresh potatoes available in shops and supermarkets throughout the year. This book is dedicated to all those who join us in celebrating that most versatile of all vegetables, the potato.

How Potatoes Are Grown

Potatoes grow practically anywhere in the world – from Greenland to Egypt, from the Arctic Circle to the tropics – but nurturing them is no easy task. Firstly, the soil has to be well prepared by ploughing every autumn, and removing stones and clods from the soil in spring, which helps to reduce bruising or damage to the potatoes when they are being harvested. The field is then fertilized. The seed potatoes must be planted on level ground in furrows and then earthed up. They need a fair, but not excessive, amount of moisture, and watering when in bloom. The rows must also be kept free of weeds. At one time many farmers were slaves to the hoe. Whole families, including children, would share the back-breaking work of growing potatoes. Today technical expertise is more essential to farmers than physical fitness, as they employ modern machinery to manage their crop. For example, a potato planter, equipped with a series of cups on an endless belt or chain, with a self-compensating device that adds a potato if an empty cup is detected, can plant up to 600 tubers under the soil every minute. The process is often supervised manually to ensure the seeds are evenly spaced, so that the crop will be a uniform size. Some farmers grow new potatoes under polythene tunnels to protect them from late frosts, and all potato growers have to guard their crops against diseases.

According to variety, each single seed potato produces up to twenty-five new tubers. Potato cultivation has become a science in its own right. If the same varieties are sown year after year their quality deteriorates, so potatoes are constantly crossbred or replaced. Specialists in plant propagation are continually creating new varieties of seed potatoes. New types of potato are designed to have not only a pleasing flavour, but also firm skins, an even size and resistance to disease. Some have to meet the needs of particular markets: the goal for many growers is to produce a larger yield in the shortest possible time, while development experts are on the

lookout for varieties suited to climatic conditions in countries of the Third World, and the food industry wants tubers with a high starch content, which are good for drying or freezing and easy to process.

It takes about ten years before a new variety is ready for the market. To achieve the desired characteristics, two types of potato plant are cross-pollinated. If pollination is successful, a new plant will grow. The seeds from its green berries are scattered in a special seed bed to produce sturdy seedlings. Of the number produced, only a tiny percentage eventually become a new variety. For example, if propagation specialists produced about a million potato seedlings, after a year, about 40,000 would survive, and after six or seven years of further selection, 40 new varieties would emerge. These would undergo around three years of further testing – including a number of tastings – by experts. After passing these tests, between eight and ten new varieties would appear on the market. The number of varieties available varies depending on where you live, but it remains constant nationally, for as new types emerge, varieties whose quality has diminished or are well past their best are withdrawn.

Misshapen and grossly oversized specimens do not stand a chance in this selection process. Only in local newspapers do we occasionally see photographs of amateur growers proudly displaying giant tubers. In recent times, genetic research has concentrated more strongly on the potato. Scientists are attempting to create potatoes 'from within', or, to be more exact, from the DNA at the heart of the plant cell.

The isolation and transfer of genes have produced tubers that are no longer prone to certain blights, which used to be treated by chemical means. Researchers are now working on the creation of the 'super-spud'. They are reported to be increasing the protein content of potatoes through genetic engineering.

From Grower to Consumer

Consumers want nice oval tubers of similar size, not necessarily very large, but with healthy, smooth, unblemished skins. To produce this result the grower has to plant the right kind of potatoes on his land. At one time potato fields were a blaze of different coloured blossoms because a mixture of seeds had been sown. Now farmers would be alarmed if their potato blossoms were the 'wrong' shade. They avoid this situation by buying fresh plants every year. Then the plants are sprouted and protected against pests and disease: nothing that can be avoided is left to chance. Even so, it is often Mother Nature herself who does the most damage. Unseasonal night frosts and rainy summers can adversely affect the quality of the crop. Tubers from the same field can vary in consistency, flavour and storage qualities from one year to the next.

Modern farmers have the harvest well organized. A single machine can do almost everything: a complete potato harvester picks the potatoes, separates them from clods of soil and lifts them on to a belt, where they are sorted. Only those who have harvested potatoes by hand will fully appreciate the benefits of such technology! Human sorters remove any remaining stones and clumps of earth, and reject any misshapen, shrivelled, bruised or damaged specimens as the tubers roll along

conveyor belts to depots, where the freshly harvested potatoes are packed and immediately transported to their various markets.

These highly mechanized harvesting techniques can be only good news for potato-lovers. Very few potatoes are damaged during lifting, and modern distribution methods mean that these light-sensitive tubers lose barely any of their nutrients. The food industry also makes good use of these

advantages. Since the 'raw material' is delivered fresh from the fields, it can be stored or carefully processed while retaining most of its goodness. We cannot expect quite so much of potatoes stored at home, even as far as flavour is concerned, because the conditions there are not as precisely controlled and, unless we are lucky enough to buy them from a farm shop, the potatoes have spent time in the distribution chain before they reach our local shops and supermarkets.

In fact, although the percentage varies, in most industrialized countries a large proportion of the annual potato crop is processed. For example, in Australia, which grows 1.1 million tonnes of potatoes annually, about 49 per cent is used for processing; Britain, which produces about 7.5 million tonnes a year, sends about 37 per cent directly to food manufacturers; while Germany, which harvests over 10 million tonnes in a year, delivers about 33 per cent to the food-processing industry. In

whatever form we eat them, potatoes are still one of our favourite foods. It is interesting to note that Ireland, which has been a potato-loving nation since the seventeenth century, still leads the world in per capita consumption, at 140 kg (309 lb) a year. Elsewhere the potato competes with rice and pasta as a major carbohydrate and a 'fast food', but annual per capita consumption in Britain is still about 100 kg (220 lb), and in Australia about 63.5 kg (140 lb).

Potatoes Are So Healthy

Every potato is a power pack, brimming with goodness. In theory, we could eat only potatoes, supplemented with the occasional glass of milk or the odd egg (to provide animal protein), and the body would suffer no dietary deficiency. As we are in the happy position of enjoying a far more mixed diet, we do not eat enough potatoes. This is a pity, say health practitioners, listing all the good things to be found in potatoes.

Potatoes are full of vitamins

Potatoes contain Vitamins C, B1 (thiamine), B2 (riboflavin), B3 and B6 (pyridoxine). The most important of these is Vitamin C. The entire recommended daily amount for an adult can be found in 400 g (14 oz) of potatoes. The vitamin content is at its peak at harvest time, and decreases during storage. More vitamins disappear during cooking. Potatoes boiled in their skins and large baked potatoes lose about 20–40 per cent of their Vitamin C alone, while chips and roast potatoes lose about 30–40 per cent, and peeled, boiled potatoes lose as much as 30–50 per cent.

Potatoes contain high-grade protein

The quality of protein we consume matters more than the quantity. Potato protein is an ideal blend of essential amino acids. Since the body functions most efficiently on a mixture of vegetable and animal proteins, from a health point of view the best combination is potato protein with milk or egg, such as creamy mashed potatoes with a fried egg or fried potatoes with scrambled egg.

Potatoes are rich in minerals

The potato's high potassium content means it is an ideal way to offset the surplus acid in such foods as meat and certain kinds of vegetables. Many people (women more than men) suffer from iron and magnesium deficiencies, particularly those who take part in a lot of sport. Those who eat potatoes on a regular basis have no need to take iron or magnesium supplements.

Potatoes are low in calories

Many people would be surprised to learn that 100 g (3 ½ oz) of boiled potatoes contain only 75–80 calories. Even chips, which contain 230 calories per 100 g (3 ½ oz) because of the fat in which they are cooked, have less than half the number of calories in a piece of chocolate cake of the same weight. If you ate nothing but potatoes, you would have to consume almost 3 kg (6 ½ lb) of boiled potatoes or 1 kg (2 ⅕ lb) of chips a day in order to meet a daily requirement of 2200 calories!

Potatoes contain complex carbohydrates

It used to be unjustly claimed that carbohydrates led to excess weight. We now know that they are the body's most important source of energy. Among the complex carbohydrates are starch and fibre. During the digestive process cooked potato starch is converted into carbohydrate and stored as an energy reserve in the liver and muscles. Fibre is a vital aid to digestion. It absorbs a great deal of body fluid and expands enormously. This increased bulk encourages more efficient bowel function. Fibre-rich foods stay in the system only half as long as those with little fibre. Most importantly, fibre enables the body to expel far more quickly harmful substances absorbed from the environment, as well as the body's own toxins and waste products.

Potatoes are very low in fat

The fat content of potatoes is only 0.01–0.1 per cent. This tiny quantity includes 'good' essential fatty acids.

Potato Diets and Remedies

Some doctors and health practitioners recommend a potato-rich diet to people with various illnesses.

The potato diet
We are warned against many diets, not because they allow too little food, but because the choice of what to eat is so limited. No danger of this with the potato diet! Although you are eating less than usual, potatoes are so nutritious that the body gets all the nourishment it needs. You will not go hungry either: since potatoes are so low in calories, on a daily allowance of 1000 calories you can eat your fill. If you divide 600 g (1 ¼ lb) of potatoes between your midday and evening meals, you will still have just about 500 calories to spare for a variety of other food, and for breakfast. The potato diet has another virtue: the high potassium content helps the body flush away excess fluid.

Diabetes
Many diabetics are overweight. Their bodies must have a steady supply of carbohydrates, but not in excessive quantities, to avoid creating too much sugar in the blood. On a potato diet, diabetics can lose weight without any harmful side-effects.

Kidney deficiency
To avoid having to resort to dialysis, people whose kidneys fail to excrete waste products must eat little protein, which must be of high quality. Because of its biological efficiency, the potato and egg diet is especially good for kidney patients.

Gout
Gout, the so called 'rich man's complaint', is caused mainly by consuming too much meat and animal fat. One of the symptoms is the overproduction of uric acid. The most important part of treatment is a diet low in this acid. Potatoes contain very little uric acid and therefore can be the main ingredient in an anti-gout diet.

High blood pressure
When certain bodily functions are disturbed, the kidneys excrete insufficient sodium, which leads to raised blood pressure (hypertension). Sufferers are prescribed an extremely low-sodium diet. This means eating foods naturally low in sodium and avoiding or restricting the use of salt in their preparation. Potatoes are the perfect low-sodium food, so patients with high blood pressure are urged to include frequent 'potato days' in their diet.

Coeliac disease
So far no cure has been found for this intolerance of any type of grain. Sufferers find potatoes easy to take, and can make them the mainstay of their diet.

Potatoes as a home remedy
Not everyone wants to carry a potato in their pocket or hang one around their neck to ward off rheumatism – even though the Incas are reported to have found it helpful. Here are a few proven, easy-to-follow home remedies.

For diarrhoea, eat unsalted potatoes mashed with water.

For heartburn and wind, drink freshly squeezed juice of raw potatoes first thing in the morning (some practitioners of alternative medicine even prescribe this treatment for stomach ulcers).

For stomach pain and sore throat, make a compress by placing hot, unpeeled, boiled potatoes in a linen bag, or wrap them in a tea-towel. Crush them coarsely, then apply to the affected part.

*Buying and
Storing
Potatoes*

Potatoes are carefully cleaned, sorted and graded before they reach the shops and supermarkets to ensure that you find only healthy, firm potatoes with smooth skins. The slight green patches on potato skins sometimes seen in supermarkets are caused by exposure to light and sometimes by the temperature at which they are stored or displayed. This kind of greening is usually superficial and easily removed by peeling. (Darker greening, which happens when potatoes are exposed to light while they are growing, is unhealthy, and affected potatoes are normally discarded during sorting.) Potatoes are also sensitive to damp, so you should not accept those displayed outdoors if they have been exposed to rain.

The plastic bags in which potatoes are often sold are not a brilliant idea. As the temperature fluctuates, the potatoes sweat, and can become mouldy. If this is the most convenient way for you to buy them, transfer them to an open basket or a paper bag as soon as you get them home.

Buy potatoes in quantities that you plan to use within a short period of time. Store them in a cool, dark place with good air circulation, not in the refrigerator.

If you are planning to peel the potatoes before cooking, do so only when your are ready to use them: peeled potatoes that are kept sitting in water lose more of their nutrients than those that are peeled and cooked immediately.

Utensils

The following pages show very useful kitchen tools designed for tackling potatoes.

Cook's knife

Potato peelers

Paring knife

Vegetable knife

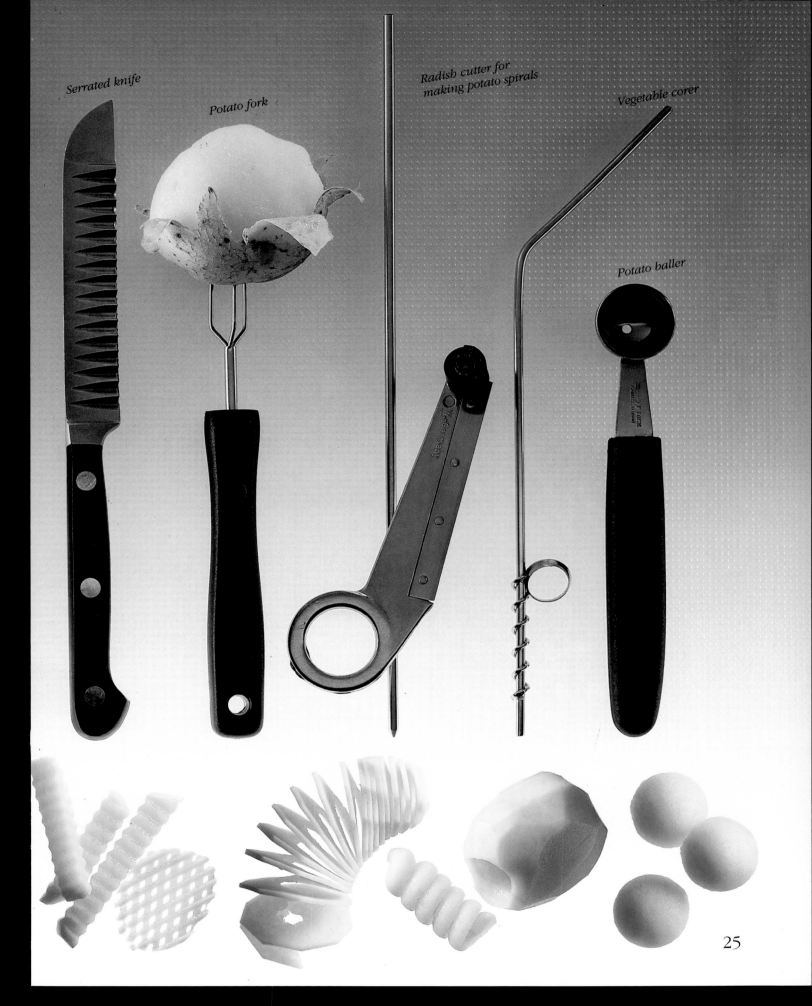

Serrated knife

Potato fork

Radish cutter for
making potato spirals

Vegetable corer

Potato baller

25

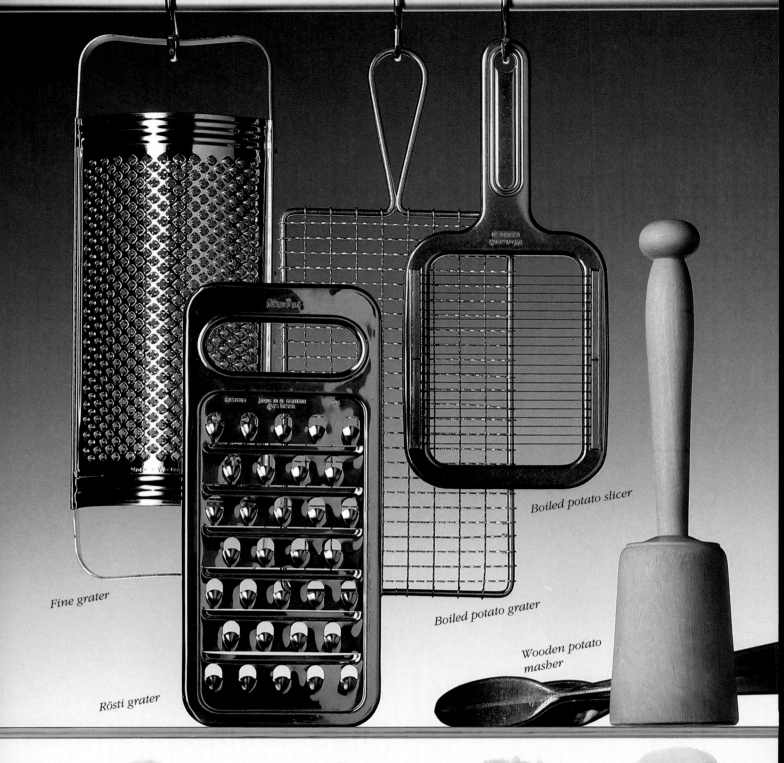

Fine grater

Rösti grater

Boiled potato slicer

Boiled potato grater

Wooden potato masher

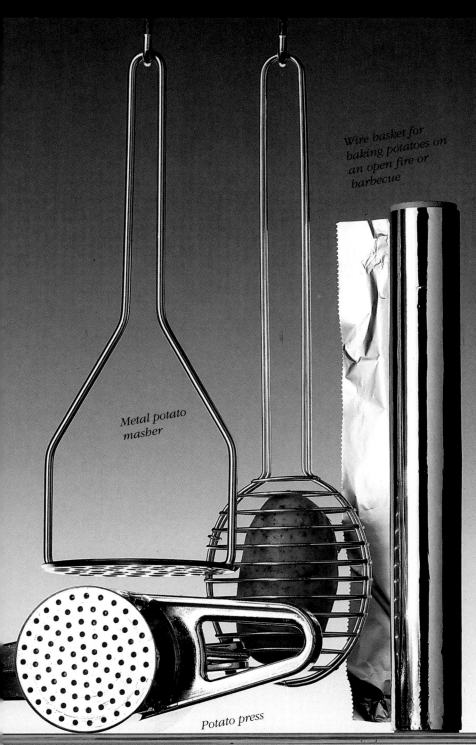

Metal potato masher

Wire basket for baking potatoes on an open fire or barbecue

Potato press

Cooking is much more fun — and takes less time — if you have the right equipment to hand. Apart from their usefulness, simple, shiny utensils displayed on a rack are an aesthetic delight for many cooks, and quite the nicest way to decorate a kitchen wall. The choice of tools depends on individual need and personal taste. If you never prepare potato purée, a masher is, of course, unnecessary. On the other hand, if you like to experiment, the right utensils will broaden your scope. Take the examples on page 25: we have used a vegetable corer from Spain and a radish cutter from Germany on raw potatoes. The result is amusing potato spirals, which, when deep-fried, make an interesting change from straight-cut chips.

Slotted ladle

Chip ladle

Whisk

Double chip
basket for
potato nests

Chip basket

28

All You Need for Deep-Frying

Deep fryer

If you are a lover of fried foods, it is worth investing in a deep-fryer. This keeps the fat at the constant high temperature needed for frying. The hotter the fat, the quicker the food will cook, and the less fat it will absorb, which means it will contain fewer calories.

Chip cutter

SAFRAN

Glossary

The potato's own mild flavour blends perfectly with a wide range of spices and strong-tasting herbs. It is best not to use too great a mixture, however. Add generous quantities, but only one herb or spice at a time, so that its flavour really penetrates.

Allspice

This pungent spice is made from unripe allspice berries. Not only is the flavour peppery, it also has hints of cloves, nutmeg and cinnamon. Allspice is used in the same way as these three spices.

Bay leaves

Fresh leaves of the evergreen bay tree or bush are more aromatic than when dried, the form in which they are most often used. If you particularly enjoy their strong, slightly bitter taste, you could plant a tree for yourself. Bay leaves tend to be used too sparingly; instead of half a leaf, you can quite happily add two or three to soups or stews.

Capers

These flower buds of a Mediterranean bush are made edible by pickling in brine or vinegar. The smaller they are, the more subtle their flavour. Their sharp, bitter flavour makes them ideal for substantial potato salads, and they also add a distinctive tang to mixed salads.

Caraway

The seed of a plant with finely divided leaves and small, whitish flowers, caraway is used to flavour hearty dishes. The taste is pleasant but strong, so caraway seeds should be used sparingly, with one exception: you can add a healthy dose to the water when boiling potatoes in their skins, so that the flavour can penetrate the skins.

Cardamom

This plant, which is a relative of ginger, is grown mainly in south-east Asia, and its dried seed pods are used in cooking. To retain their sweetish, resinous taste, buy whole pods and crush them in a pestle and mortar when you need them. Exotic cardamom may seem an unusual ingredient to combine with potatoes, but why not give it a try?

Cayenne pepper

Made from ground red chilli peppers, cayenne is hot and aromatic. Buy it only in small quantities and use it quickly, as it soon loses its flavour but retains its nip. Use cayenne in hot and spicy dishes such as potato bread.

Chervil

A delicate herb that can be grown in a pot, and is most aromatic in spring and autumn. Fresh chervil leaves have a slightly sweet, aniseed flavour. Chervil adds a distinctive note to potato soup, and is good in springtime with new potatoes.

Chilli peppers

Fresh chilli peppers are spicy; dried ones are simply hot. The rule is the smaller the peppers, the more fiery they are. Finely chopped or crushed with a pestle and mortar, they add extra zest to fried potatoes. Preserved chillies — often labelled *pepperoni* — are best used straight out of the jar; they are not very good for cooking. In the pickling process they take on a slightly sour flavour as well as their characteristic fieriness.

Chives

Easy to grow in a pot or garden, chives have an onion flavour and can be used in all savoury dishes. To bring out their fresh tang, snip them with kitchen scissors and sprinkle over food just before serving; they should not be cooked. For a change, you can arrange a bunch of fine stems on top of the finished dish. Chive flowers also make an attractive decoration.

Cinnamon

This commonly used spice is the bark of a type of bay tree growing in Asia, which rolls up as it is peeled from the tree. The thinner the bark is shaved, the more delicate the cinnamon flavour. The finest and sweetest cinnamon comes from Sri Lanka and is sold in sticks. Other varieties of cinnamon, usually rather more bitter and spicy, are usually ground. As well as using cinnamon for cakes and desserts, small quantities can be added to sweet-and-sour dishes.

Cloves

Looking like tiny nails, cloves are the flowerbuds of a huge tropical tree. They must be picked before the flowers open. Because of their strong perfume and slightly woody flavour, they should be used sparingly.

Dill

This herb, with its feathery leaves, is available dried, but is even tastier fresh. Dill best retains its characteristic flavour when raw, or cooked only briefly. It is good with potato salad, or simply sprinkled over boiled potatoes. In Sweden smoked salmon is often served accompanied by potatoes in a béchamel and dill sauce.

Garlic

If you like garlic, you can add it to anything — except desserts. The problem for most people is the lingering odour. Nobody has yet found a really effective remedy, although chewing fresh parsley after eating garlic is said to help. It is also important to know that the younger and fresher the garlic, the more subtle the flavour and the less persistent the smell. True garlic lovers can add generous amounts, sliced or crushed in a garlic press, to fried potatoes, casseroles and potato salads. If you prefer only a hint of garlic, rub the salad bowl or frying-pan with a cut clove.

Juniper berries

The berries are gathered from wild juniper bushes (related to the cypress tree). The smaller the berries, the better the sharp, bitter-sweet flavour. They add interest to marinades and sauces. Juniper berries should be crushed before use. Do not use more than about three berries per person, otherwise the taste is overpowering.

Marjoram

It is marjoram that gives black pudding and liver sausage their characteristic taste. Since dried marjoram has such a good flavour, it is seldom used fresh, although it is so much more delicious. Good in potato soup, marjoram also adds interest to fried and roast potatoes.

Mustard seeds

The white and black seeds have no smell. They acquire their characteristic hot mustardy taste only when soaked in water. Whole mustard seeds can be used to season dressings for potato salads and similar dishes.

Nutmeg

The term 'nut' is misleading. Botanically speaking, nutmeg is the seed of the nutmeg tree, which grows to a height of up to 16 metres (52 feet). The dried kernel is grated before use. Mace is the name given to the outer covering of the nutmeg. It has the same fragrance and the same spicy flavour as nutmeg, but is more intense. Nutmeg is sold whole or ground. It is a must for mashed potatoes, and is also delicious in potato gratins and gnocchi.

Oregano

Marjoram's wild relative, oregano grows around the Mediterranean and is sold dried. Oregano can be used in the same dishes as marjoram.

Paprika

Dried peppers are ground to produce paprika. The more seeds and ribs that are used with the dried flesh, the hotter the flavour and the brighter the colour. The label of some brands indicates mild, sweet or hot. Sweet paprika is aromatic with very little fieriness. Hot paprika has a pungent taste. The milder types of paprika turn bitter when fried, so it is best to use them in stews such as potato goulash.

Parsley

This is probably the most universal and most commonly used culinary herb. Flat-leaved parsley has a stronger flavour than the curly variety, and both are easy to grow in the garden or in a flowerpot on the windowsill. One of its classic uses is in parsley potatoes.

Pepper

There are three different types of pepper. Black pepper berries are picked while still unripe, then dried. They have a hot and fiery taste. White pepper is made from ripe, peeled berries of the pepper plant, and has a milder flavour. Green pepper berries are also picked before they are ripe, and can be used fresh, pickled or freeze-dried. They have a mild and very aromatic flavour. So-called 'pink pepper' is not really pepper at all, but a member of the elderberry family. The flavour is hot and peppery, with a hint of sweetness.
In order to retain both the spiciness and fragrance of pepper, grind the peppercorns over the food just before serving.

Rosemary

In appearance and aroma rosemary is rather similar to pine needles. It adds distinctive flavour fresh or dried. The dry leaves remain fairly hard even when cooked. If this is not to your taste, you may prefer to crush them, using a pestle and mortar. Rosemary is good with all types of Mediterranean summer dishes, and is also delicious with pan-fried or roast potatoes.

Saffron

Since harvesting the delicate stigmas of the saffron crocus is done by hand, and is exceptionally laborious and not very productive, saffron is extremely expensive. There are many imitations on the market. You can avoid them to some extent by refusing to buy saffron in powdered form. Saffron has a strong smell and a slightly bitter taste. Used even in tiny quantities, it gives food a bright yellow colour, making potato dishes look quite exotic.

Sage

The characteristic taste of the grey-green, silvery leaves gives any dish an "Italian" flavour. Crisply fried in hot fat, sage is particularly delicious. Try sprinkling it over pan-fried potatoes.

Savory

With a perfume similar to thyme, savory has a bitter, peppery flavour, which is most intense when the plant is just beginning to flower. It is then picked and dried. Savory is good in hearty potato soups and casseroles.

Thyme

The small thyme leaves have a powerful, slightly bitter taste, and do not lose any of their flavour when dried. In addition to common garden thyme, various types are grown for use in refined dishes, including lemon, orange and caraway thyme. They provide novel flavours for potato dishes.

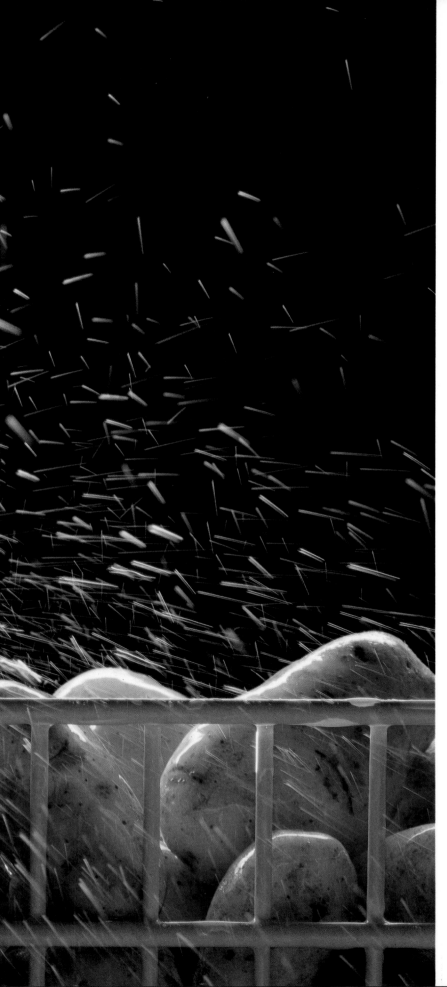

New Potatoes

For many of us the nicest thing about springtime is the arrival of new potatoes. While some people's thoughts immediately turn to asparagus, for others the best treat of all is a plateful of potatoes, with a little butter and salt, and nothing else.

New potatoes are sensitive creatures and must be handled with care. They should be neither peeled nor scrubbed, but simply rinsed under running water. With their paper-thin skins, they take less time to cook than older potatoes. Just place them in a pot of boiling water and they will be ready in an average of 15 minutes. The skin of new potatoes is a delicacy in itself. Although new potatoes have only a short season, it is best not to stock up on them, as their appearance soon spoils. Just buy them as you need them and enjoy them as fresh as possible.

Potatoes Provençal

1 ½ kg (3 ½ lb) small new potatoes

6 tbsp olive oil

60 g (2 oz) butter

salt

leaves from 3 stems of sage

leaves from 3 stems of marjoram

2 cloves garlic, chopped

2 tsp sugar

Leave the potatoes unpeeled and wash them clean, then dry thoroughly with kitchen towels.

Heat the olive oil in a heavy-based frying-pan, then lightly brown the potatoes, stirring constantly.

Reduce the heat and stir in the butter, salt, herbs and garlic.

Stirring constantly and shaking the pan, fry the potatoes until golden brown.

The potatoes are done when they are tender enough to be pierced with a fork.

Sprinkle the sugar over the potatoes and cook until caramelized.

Season to taste with salt and serve piping hot.

Serves 4
227 calories per serving
Recommended salads: 5, 3

Asparagus and Parma Ham with Parsley Potatoes

2 kg (4 ½ lb) white asparagus

juice of 1 lemon

200 g (7 oz) butter

1 tsp sugar

200 g (7 oz) thinly sliced Parma ham

Peel the asparagus, cutting off the woody ends.

Bring a pan full of water to the boil with the lemon juice, butter and sugar.

Add the asparagus and cook for about 15 minutes.

Serve with Parma ham and new potatoes boiled in their skins and drenched in butter and finely chopped parsley.

Serves 4
625 calories per serving

Boiled Potatoes

For meat and fish dishes served with an exquisite sauce, there is no better accompaniment than boiled potatoes. Their velvety consistency enables them to absorb the sauce without impairing the flavour. Here is the best way to prepare boiled potatoes.

Peel the potatoes as thinly as possible, removing eyes and blemishes, then rinse and place them in cold salted water. The less water used, the more vitamins the potatoes will retain. As soon as the water comes to the boil, turn the heat down so that it is just enough to keep the pan bubbling. After 20 minutes, test the potatoes by piercing them with a fork or the point of a knife. If they are soft all the way through, then they are done. If necessary, for larger potatoes, cook for a few minutes longer. Drain off the water, then, leaving the lid off, return the saucepan to the heat and shake it gently a couple of times, making sure the potatoes do not burn.

Potatoes in Paradise

With only minimum effort, you can prepare a meal like this to please even the most demanding guest. First boil some really good-quality potatoes in their skins, then surround them with a selection of ingredients, from the refined to the substantial, from caviare to the humble onion. Simply anything tastes wonderful with potatoes boiled in their skins!

Beluga caviare

Watercress

Cream cheese

Sevruga caviare

Spring onion

Lime

Parsley

Hard-boiled egg

Chives

Onion

Butter

Crème fraîche

Salmon caviare

Radish

Smoked salmon

Dill

Herb butter

Rollmop herring

Recommended salad: 1

Potato Salads

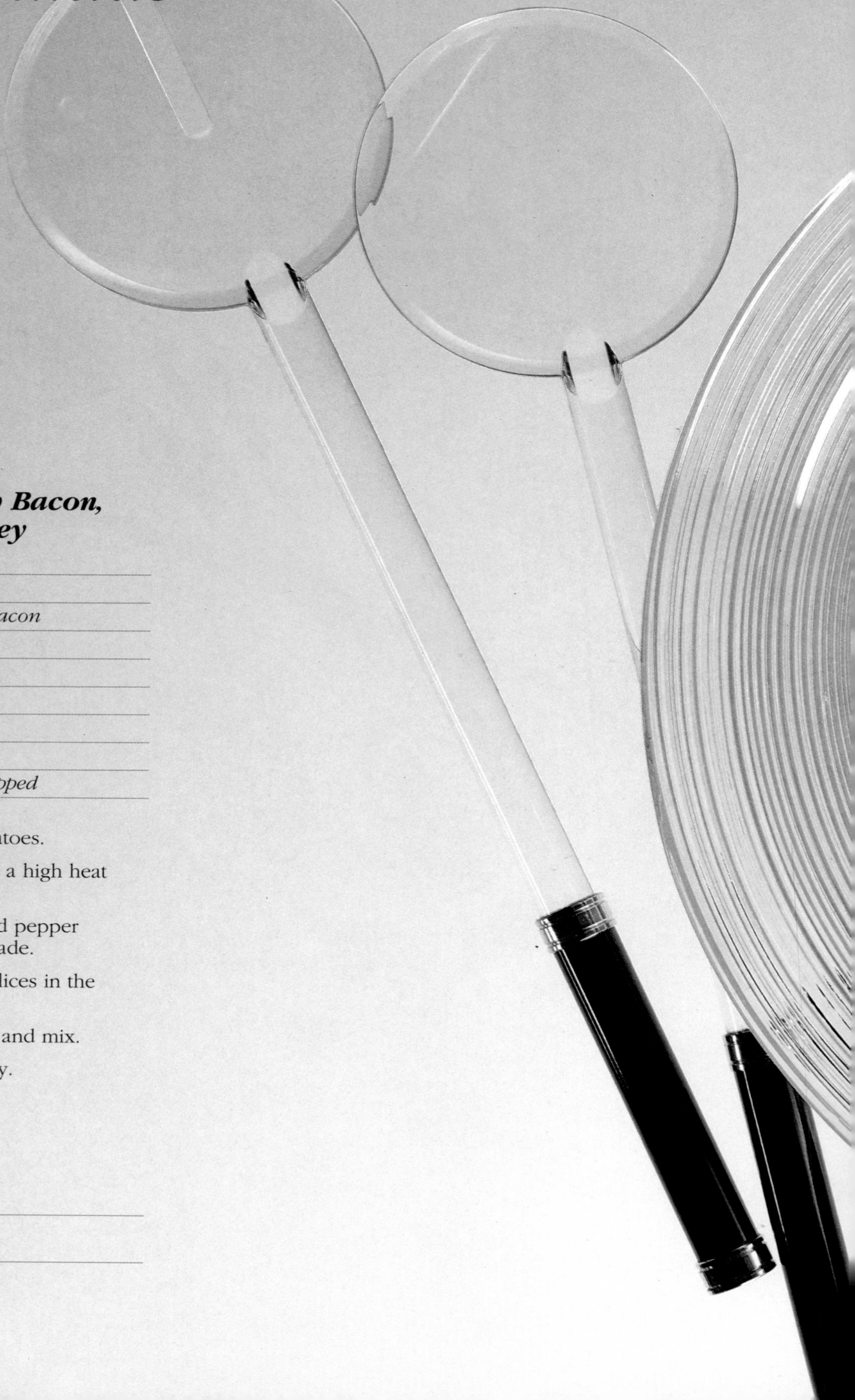

Potato Salad with Bacon, Onions and Parsley

1 kg (2 lb) potatoes

200 g (7 oz) slab smoked bacon

4 tbsp vinegar

12 tbsp oil

salt

freshly ground pepper

3 onions, diced

1 bunch parsley, finely chopped

Peel, boil and slice the potatoes.

Dice the bacon and fry it at a high heat until crispy.

Mix the vinegar, oil, salt and pepper together to make the marinade.

Carefully place the potato slices in the marinade.

Add the bacon and onions, and mix.

Serve garnished with parsley.

Serves 4
635 calories per serving

44

Potato Salad with Apples and Almonds

1 kg (2 ¼ lb) waxy potatoes, boiled in their skins	
2 white onions	
100 g (3 ½ oz) peeled almonds	
450 g (1 lb) red apples	
juice of 1 lemon	
2 egg yolks	
115–225 ml (4–8 fl oz) walnut oil	
115 ml (4 fl oz) double cream, whipped	
2 tbsp apple juice	
3 tbsp cider vinegar	
salt	
freshly ground pepper	

Peel the potatoes while still warm, then slice.

Peel and slice the onions.

Halve the almonds and toast in a dry frying-pan.

Cut the apples into quarters, core, and sprinkle with lemon juice.

Beat the egg yolks until frothy, then gradually add the oil to make mayonnaise.

Fold in the cream, apple juice and vinegar, and season with salt and pepper.

Carefully mix the onions, almonds and apples, and toss in the mayonnaise.

Potato Salad with Cheese and Olives

1 kg (2 ¼ lb) waxy organic potatoes, boiled in their skins
12 tbsp olive oil
1 sprig rosemary
1 white onion, finely chopped
1 egg yolk
3 tbsp vinegar
salt
freshly ground pepper
2 beef tomatoes, skinned and deseeded
200 g (7 oz) ewe's milk cheese
100 g (3 ½ oz) black olives
leaves of 1 sprig rosemary

Peel the potatoes while still warm.

Heat the olive oil in a frying-pan, and brown the rosemary and onions. Drain off and reserve the oil.

Beat the egg yolk until frothy, then add the oil a little at a time to make mayonnaise.

Season to taste with vinegar, salt and pepper.

Dice the tomatoes, slice the potatoes and crumble the cheese.

Carefully stir the onions, tomatoes, olives, cheese and rosemary into the mayonnaise.

Serve sprinkled with rosemary.

Pan-Fried Potatoes

Nearly every fried-potato fan has his or her own special recipe. Nevertheless, they all agree on a few ground rules. Waxy or firm-textured potatoes are best, since they retain their shape. Do not use butter or virgin olive oil, as they cannot be heated to a high enough temperature. Neutral-tasting vegetable oil or fat, or clarified butter, is good for frying potatoes, and so are pork and goose dripping, if you like the taste.

Raw potatoes for frying should be sliced or diced. Heat the fat in the biggest available frying-pan. Add the potatoes and reduce the heat to medium. Pan-fried potatoes turn out best when they have plenty of room to move in the pan. They should not overlap. Most important of all: be patient! It takes at least 20 minutes to cook raw potatoes in a frying-pan to be sure they are tender and crunchy. Turn them over only when the underside is nice and crisp. Too much stirring and turning will only make them mushy and shapeless. Onions should be added to the pan after about 10 minutes. Wait until the potatoes are done before sprinkling them with salt, pepper and herbs. For a touch of luxury, melt a generous pat of butter over them just before serving.

Fried Eggs

15 g (½ oz) butter

1 tbsp oil

4 eggs

salt

freshly ground pepper

1 bunch chives, finely chopped

Gently heat the butter and oil in a frying-pan. Do not let the fat get too hot.

Slide the eggs into the pan and fry slowly.

Season with salt and pepper, and sprinkle with chives.

Pan-Fried Potatoes

1 kg (2 ¼ lb) waxy potatoes, boiled in their skins in advance

80 g (3 oz) clarified butter

salt

freshly ground pepper

Peel the pre-cooked, cold potatoes and cut into fairly thick slices.

Heat the clarified butter in a heavy-based frying-pan, then add the potatoes.

Brown the potatoes over a high heat, but do not turn them too often. Pre-cooked potatoes must be fried over a high heat, otherwise they will brown too slowly and the insides will become leathery.

Finally, season with salt and pepper right at the end. If salt is added too soon the potatoes will absorb moisture and will not brown.

Serves 4
456 calories per serving
Recommended salads: 1, 3

Sausage Ring

15 g (½ oz) butter

1 tbsp oil

1 large bratwurst or other sausage

Heat the butter and oil in a frying-pan.

Roll the sausage into a spiral and secure with a wooden skewer.

Add the sausage to the frying-pan.

Fry for about 5 minutes on each side.

Baste occasionally with fat.

Serve with Pan-Fried Potatoes.

Serves 4
133 calories per serving
Recommended salad: 3

Summer Vegetable Mould in Aspic with Cucumber

1 bunch white baby turnips
1 bunch spring carrots
500 g (1 lb) broccoli
1 medium-sized cauliflower
200 g (7 oz) haricots verts
35 g (1 ¼ oz) gelatine
1 l (2 pt) strongly flavoured instant vegetable stock
115 ml (4 fl oz) dry sherry
1 cucumber
15 g (½ oz) butter
dill, finely chopped
100 ml (3 ½ fl oz) white wine
salt
freshly ground pepper

Clean and peel the vegetables. Cut the turnips and carrots into strips. Divide the broccoli and cauliflower into florets. Top and tail the beans.

Cook the vegetables separately in salted water or steam until tender but still crisp. Drain in a colander and rinse under cold water. Dry thoroughly on kitchen towels.

Soak the gelatine in 8 tablespoons cold water for 4 minutes. Heat the stock and sherry, then dissolve the gelatine in the liquid.

Pour a little stock into a terrine dish. Place in the refrigerator until set. Add the carrots, then carefully cover with more stock. Repeat the process with each of the vegetables, allowing each layer to set before adding the next layer of vegetables.

Chill the terrine in the refrigerator for 5–6 hours.

Peel the cucumber and cut into sticks.

Heat the butter and sauté the cucumber. Add the dill and wine, and season to taste with salt and pepper.

Cut the mould into slices and serve with the cucumber and Pan-Fried Potatoes.

Serves 4
227 calories per serving
Recommended salads: 5, 3

Pot Roast with Vegetables

1 kg (2 ¼ lb) leg of beef

3–4 beef bones

1 bunch soup vegetables, such as leek,
carrot and celery

1 tsp salt

1 peeled parsley root, if available

3 peppercorns

2 bay leaves

1 onion spiked with 4 cloves

2 leeks

1 bunch carrots

1 bunch white baby turnips

1 small head celeriac

Place the meat and bones in a large
saucepan with enough cold water to cover.
Bring to the boil over a medium heat,
skimming off the scum.

Turn down the heat and add the soup
vegetables, salt, parsley root, peppercorns,
bay leaves and onion.

Simmer gently for 3 hours.

Leave the meat to cool in the broth, then
strain the broth, reserving it and the meat
separately.

Trim and wash the leek and carrots. Peel
the turnips and the celeriac. Cut the leek
diagonally into pieces. Cut the celeriac into
eight sections. Leave the carrots and turnips
whole.

Add the vegetables to the broth and cook
for 20 minutes until tender.

Thinly slice the beef and serve with the
vegetables and Pan-Fried Potatoes.

Optional

Freshly grated horseradish

Apple and horseradish sauce (a mixture of
equal quantities of grated apple and
horseradish)

Chive sauce (crème fraîche mixed with
chives and seasoned with salt and pepper)

Serves 4
299 calories per serving
Recommended salad: 6

Veal in Mushroom Sauce

600 g (1 ¼ lb) thin escalopes of veal	
2 tbsp oil	
25 g (1 oz) butter	
1 onion, finely chopped	
200 g (7 oz) button mushrooms, thinly sliced	
1 bunch tarragon, finely chopped	
200 ml (7 fl oz) white wine	
200 ml (7 fl oz) single cream	
salt	
freshly ground pepper	

Cut the escalopes into thin strips about 6 cm (2 ½ in) long.

Heat the oil in a frying-pan, and brown the meat in batches. Drain the meat through a sieve, reserving the juices.

Heat the butter in the pan, and sauté the onion and mushrooms. Stir in the tarragon. Add the wine, bring to the boil and reduce the liquid slightly. Add the cream and meat juices, then reduce to a creamy sauce.

Return the meat to the pan and heat through. Season to taste with salt and pepper.

Serve the veal with wedges of Rösti.

Rösti

800 g (1 ¾ lb) waxy potatoes boiled in their skins the day before	
salt	
3 tbsp oil	
40 g (1 ½ oz) butter	

Peel the potatoes, grate coarsely, and season with salt.

Heat the oil and butter in a non-stick frying-pan, add the rösti and fry over a medium heat until golden, pressing the potatoes flat in the frying-pan.

Cover the rösti with a plate, turn the pan and plate upside down, then slide the rösti back into the pan. Fry the other side until crisp and golden.

Serves 4
588 calories per serving

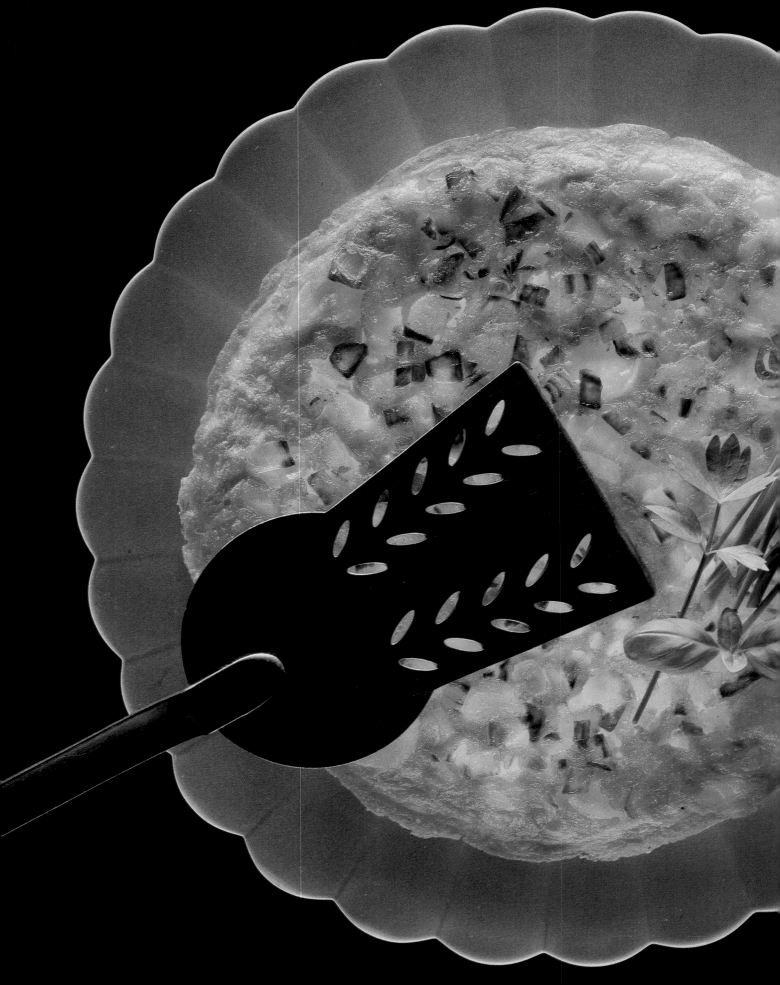

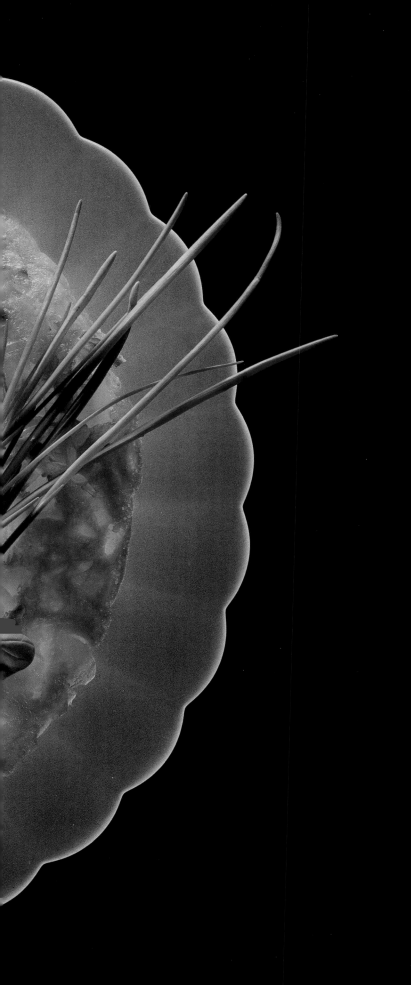

Potato and Onion Tortilla

200 g (7 oz) onions

400 g (14 oz) potatoes

6 tbsp olive oil

salt

freshly ground pepper

6 eggs

Peel and dice the onions.

Peel the potatoes and cut into 2-cm (1-in) cubes.

Heat 4 tablespoons of the oil in a frying-pan and fry the onions until transparent.

Add the potatoes and cook for about 15 minutes until soft, turning occasionally.

Season with salt and pepper.

Beat the eggs until frothy, add salt and pour over the potatoes. Allow to thicken, turning frequently. Place a lid on the frying-pan and cook on a low heat until golden yellow, shaking occasionally.

Cover the tortilla with a plate and turn it and the pan upside-down. Place the remaining oil in the pan, slide the tortilla into it and cook on a low heat, with the lid off, until golden.

Serves 4
242 calories per serving
Recommended salad: 4

Soups

Creamy, textured potato soups
are traditional favourites. Now
the latest invention and a small
culinary miracle, clear potato
soup is a perfect example of the
versatility of the potato. If you are
serving potato soup as a starter,
use only the finest ingredients, as
illustrated in the following pages.

Potato Consommé with Crayfish

12 crayfish
1 courgette
1 red radish
2 carrots
2 tomatoes, peeled and deseeded
1 kg (2 ¼ lb) floury-to-firm potatoes
2 tbsp oil
1 l (2 pt) beef consommé
salt
freshly ground pepper
leaves of 2 sprigs basil

Simmer the crayfish in boiling salted water for 4 minutes.

Drain in a colander, allow to cool, then remove the shells.

Trim and wash the courgette, radish and carrots, then cut them into finger-length sticks. Dice the tomatoes.

Peel the potatoes, slice half of them, and cut the rest into thin strips. Cook the vegetables and potatoes separately until tender but still crisp, drain in a colander and rinse under cold running water.

Heat the oil in a frying-pan and fry the sliced potatoes until crisp and brown.

Add the beef consommé and simmer gently for 10 minutes.

Strain through a sieve and season to taste with salt and pepper.

Add the potato strips and vegetable strips to the soup, then reheat gently.

Divide the crayfish between 4 plates, and pour the soup over them.

Serve garnished with basil leaves.

Serves 4
440 calories per serving

German-Style Potato Soup

1 kg (2 ¼ lb) waxy potatoes

100 g (3 ½ oz) butter

1/4 head of celeriac, diced

1 diced carrot

1 leek, cut lengthways into strips, then sliced crossways

1 diced onion

225 ml (8 fl oz) single cream

salt

freshly ground pepper

nutmeg

4 slices white bread

100 g (3 ½ oz) slab smoked bacon

1 fresh garlic stalk or 1 spring onion, cut diagonally into thin strips

Peel and coarsely dice the potatoes

Heat 55 g (2 oz) of the butter in a large saucepan. Sauté the potatoes, celeriac and carrots in the butter, then cover with cold water.

Simmer over a low heat for 40 minutes.

Pass half the soup through a sieve, mashing the potatoes and vegetables to a purée. Heat 15 g (½ oz) of butter in a frying-pan and sauté the leek and onion, add to the purée, then combine with the rest of the soup.

Add the cream and simmer for about 5 minutes, then season to taste with salt, pepper and nutmeg.

To make croûtons, dice the bread, heat the remaining butter in a frying-pan and fry the bread until golden brown.

Dice the bacon and brown in the butter-coated frying-pan.

Serve the soup sprinkled with croûtons, diced bacon and garlic stalk or spring onion.

Serves 4
670 calories per serving

Potato Soup with Truffles

450 g (1 lb) floury potatoes

200 ml (7 fl oz) single cream

200 g (7 oz) butter

salt

freshly ground pepper

nutmeg

570 ml (1 pt) highly seasoned beef
  consommé

40 g (3 ½ oz) black or white truffles

leaves from 1 sprig watercress or purslane

Peel 350 g (12 oz) potatoes, cook in salted
water for about 20 minutes, then drain in a
colander.

Mash them to a smooth purée with the
cream and half the butter.

Season with salt, pepper and nutmeg. Add
the consommé and bring to the boil. Stir
thoroughly with a whisk.

Peel and finely dice the remaining
potatoes.

Clarify the rest of the butter. When the
butter is hot, fry the potatoes until crisp.

Scrub the truffles clean.

Add the fried potatoes to the soup and
reheat gently.

Serve garnished with finely sliced truffles
and watercress or purslane leaves.

Serves 4
620 calories per serving

Potato and Watercress Soup

450 g (1 lb) floury potatoes
225 ml (8 fl oz) chicken stock
225 ml (8 fl oz) double cream, stiffly whipped
salt
freshly ground pepper
100 g (3 ½ oz) butter
1 onion, finely chopped
1 bunch watercress, finely chopped

Peel the potatoes and cut them into chunks. Cook in salted water for about 15 minutes, then drain in a colander.

Mash the potatoes, then add the chicken stock and stir thoroughly.

Fold in the whipped cream and season to taste with salt and pepper.

Heat the butter in a frying-pan, sauté the onion and watercress, and add them to the soup.

Purée the soup in a blender.

Gently heat through again.

Serves 4
460 calories per serving

One-Pot Meals

There is nothing quite so satisfying as chunky stews and casseroles. These sturdier members of the soup family are packed with goodness. When temperatures start to fall outside, they really come into their own, with hearty ingredients to warm both heart and stomach. You can use any kind of meat, especially smoked specialities, which add extra flavour, but what makes theses one-pot meals so smoothly satisfying is the essential ingredient: potatoes.

Bacon, Pork and Potato Casserole

1 ½ kg (3 ½ lb) waxy potatoes
2 large onions
450 g (1 lb) thin-sliced smoked bacon
450 g (1 lb) unsmoked belly of pork
freshly ground pepper
570 ml (1 pt) single cream
225 ml (8 fl oz) white wine
pinch of cinnamon
100 g (3 ½ oz) butter, chilled and flaked
salt

Peel the potatoes and cut into slices 1 cm (½ in) thick.

Peel and slice the onions.

Remove any rind from the bacon. Line the base of a saucepan or casserole dish suitable for use on the hob with the bacon. Add the potatoes and onions.

Score a crisscross pattern in the pork rind, and season with pepper. Add to the potatoes and onions. Pour on the cream and wine.

Sprinkle with cinnamon and flakes of butter.

Place the lid on the pot, then simmer gently for 1–1 ½ hours without stirring.

Season to taste with salt and pepper.

Serves 4
194 calories per serving

Beef and Pork Stew

400 g (14 oz) leg of beef
400 g (14 oz) leg of pork
1 kg (2 ¼ lb) waxy potatoes
4 tbsp oil
salt
freshly ground pepper
½ head celeriac, peeled and diced
1 bunch carrots, diced
1 leek, cut lengthways into strips, then sliced crossways
150 g (5 oz) green beans
570 ml (1 pt) chicken stock
1 bunch parsley, finely chopped

Cut the meat into 1 ½-cm (½-in) cubes. Peel the potatoes and cut them into 1 ½-cm (½-in) cubes.

Heat the oil and fry the meat until browned all over. Season with salt and pepper.

Line the base of a large saucepan with a layer of potatoes and vegetables, then cover with a layer of meat. Continue to add alternate layers of meat and vegetables, ending with a layer of vegetables.

Pour in the chicken stock, place the lid on the pot and simmer gently for about 60 minutes.

Season to taste with salt and pepper, then serve sprinkled with chopped parsley.

Serves 4
753 calories per serving

Sausage, Leek and Potato Hotpot

1 kg (2 ¼ lb) floury to firm-textured
* potatoes*

4 leeks

40 g (1 ½ oz) butter

1 large onion, finely chopped

leaves from 1 bunch marjoram

710 ml (1 ¼ pt) chicken stock

salt

8 boiling sausages

1 bunch parsley, finely chopped

Peel and dice the potatoes.

Using only the white parts of the leeks, cut in half lengthways, then thickly slice them crossways.

Heat the butter in a large saucepan and sauté the onions and potatoes in it.

Add the leeks, marjoram and salt, and pour in the stock.

Simmer gently for about 40 minutes.

Add the sausages, then simmer for a further 15 minutes.

Serve sprinkled with parsley.

Serves 4
535 calories per serving

Potato Purées

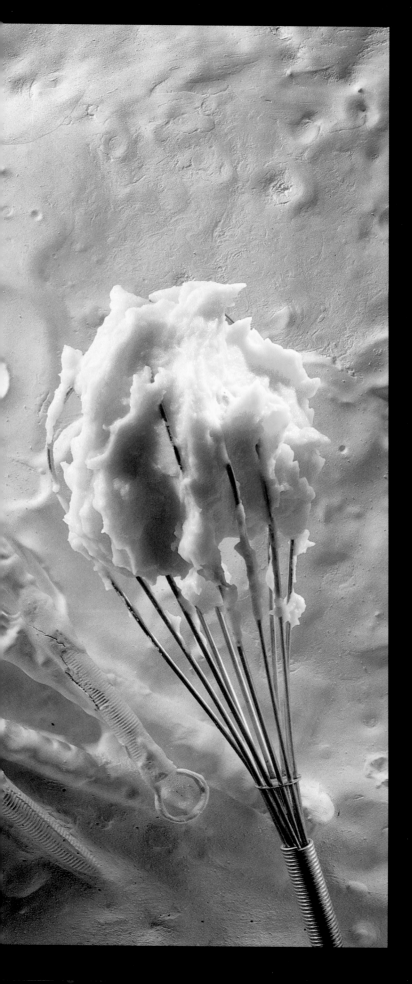

Children love potato purées, but adults too should indulge in them more often. This is the best way to prepare them: peel and boil floury or semi-floury potatoes.(You can boil them in their skins, but they will cool down too much while you peel them.) To mash the potatoes, use a potato press or pass them through a sieve with a potato masher, using firm, downward (not sideways) movements. Never use a blender or food processor: the swift circular movement extracts too much starch from the potatoes, making the purée transparent and sticky. Whether you prefer your purée completely smooth or with a few solid bits is purely a matter of individual taste. When the purée is the right consistency, gradually add boiling milk, then stir slowly with a hand whisk, until light and fluffy. At this point, season with salt, white pepper and grated nutmeg or mace. Finally, add a few flakes of butter, or a little melted butter, then serve on warm plates. Potato purée is at its best when fresh and hot!

Colourful Purées

Basic recipe

500 g (18 oz) floury potatoes
115 ml (4 fl oz) hot milk
salt
freshly ground pepper
nutmeg
50 g (2 oz) butter

Peel the potatoes and boil them in salted water for about 20 minutes.

Drain through a colander and leave to cool for a minute or two.

Mash the potatoes until smooth, add the milk and stir thoroughly with a hand whisk.

Season to taste with salt, pepper and nutmeg.

Fold in the butter.

Serves 4
202 calories per serving

Cep potato purée

50 g (2 oz) ceps
115 ml (4 fl oz) water
500 g (18 oz) potato purée
salt
freshly ground pepper
nutmeg

Soak the ceps in the water for 20 minutes, then remove, squeeze dry and chop finely.

Strain the cep water through a sieve, then boil over a high heat until reduced by half.

Stir the mushrooms and water into the hot potato purée, and season to taste with salt, pepper and nutmeg.

Serves 4
110 calories per serving

Beetroot potato purée

50 g (2 oz) butter

115 ml (4 fl oz) hot beetroot juice

500 g (18 oz) potato purée

salt

freshly ground pepper

Stir the butter and beetroot juice into the hot potato purée, and season to taste with salt and pepper.

Serves 4
211 calories per serving

Herb potato purée

small bunch chives, finely chopped

small bunch parsley, finely chopped

20 g (¾ oz) chervil, finely chopped

(add other herbs, if you like)

500 g (18 oz) potato purée

50 g (2 oz) butter

salt

freshly ground pepper

nutmeg

Add the herbs to the hot potato purée and stir thoroughly. Beat in the butter.

Season to taste with salt, pepper and nutmeg.

Serves 4
204 calories per serving

Saffron potato purée

50 g (2 oz) butter

500 g (18 oz) potato purée

4 g saffron

115 ml (4 fl oz) milk

salt

freshly ground pepper

Stir the butter into the potato purée.

Add the saffron to the milk, and bring briefly to the boil.

Stir the milk into the purée.

Season to taste with salt and pepper.

Serves 4
205 calories per serving

Turbot with Saffron Sauce and Beetroot Potato Purée

4 small turbot fillets
salt
freshly ground pepper
15 g (½ oz) butter
1 shallot, finely chopped
100 ml (3 ½ fl oz) white wine
4 g saffron
100 g (3 ½ oz) crème fraîche
100 ml (3 ½ fl oz) double cream, stiffly
    whipped

Season the fish with salt and pepper.

Grease a saucepan with butter. Sprinkle the chopped shallot over the base of the pan and arrange the fish fillets on top.

Add the wine and place the lid on the pan. Bring to the boil over a high heat, then turn the heat down low and simmer for 3 minutes.

Remove the fish from the pan and keep warm.

Add the saffron to the fish stock, then boil over a high heat until the liquid is reduced by one-third. Add the crème fraîche and reduce the sauce by half.

Carefully fold in the whipped cream, and season to taste with salt and pepper.

Serve the fish with the saffron sauce and Beetroot Potato Purée.

Serves 4
671 calories per serving

'Heaven and Earth': Potatoes and Apples with Black Pudding

1 ½ kg (3 ½ lb) floury potatoes

115 ml (4 fl oz) single cream

140 g (5 oz) butter

1 egg yolk

salt

freshly ground pepper

nutmeg

3 tbsp oil

1 black pudding ring

2 large onions, sliced

3 unpeeled, sliced apples

1 tbsp flour

Peel the potatoes, cut them into chunks and boil for about 20 minutes.

Drain in a colander and leave to cool for a few minutes.

Mash the potatoes until smooth.

Bring the cream and 100 g (3 ½ oz) of butter to the boil, then stir into the purée. Add the egg yolk.

Season to taste with salt, pepper and nutmeg.

Heat the oil in a frying-pan. Fry the black pudding for about 10 minutes, turning frequently.

Heat half the remaining butter, then fry the onions until golden brown.

Coat the apple slices in flour.

Heat the rest of the butter and fry the apple until golden brown.

Cut the black pudding into eight pieces, and arrange with the onions and apples on top of the purée.

Serves 4
832 calories per serving

Duck Breast with Shallot Butter

4 duck breasts
1 tbsp oil
130 g (4 ½ oz) butter
salt
freshly ground pepper
4 shallots, finely chopped
340 ml (12 fl oz) red wine

Pat the duck breasts dry with kitchen towels.

Heat the oil and 15 g (½ oz) of the butter in a casserole and sear the duck breasts.

Season with salt and pepper, and roast in an oven at 200°C (400°F/Gas Mark 6) for 10–15 minutes, depending on size, until pink, basting frequently.

Remove, wrap in aluminium foil and leave for 5 minutes,

Pour off the fat from the casserole, add 15 g (½ oz) butter and fry the shallots. Chill the remaining butter.

Add the red wine and cook on a high heat until the liquid has reduced by two-thirds.

Make the sauce by adding pieces of the chilled butter while beating constantly with a whisk.

Thinly slice the duck breasts and serve with the sauce.

Duchesse Potatoes

1 kg (2 ¼ lb) potatoes
100 ml (3 ½ fl oz) single cream
2 egg yolks
salt
freshly ground pepper
a little oil
nutmeg

Peel the potatoes, cut them into halves and boil in salted water for about 20 minutes.

Pour into a colander and allow to cool slightly.

Mash the potatoes.

Heat the cream and mix with the potatoes.

Add the egg yolks and stir well.

Season with salt, pepper and nutmeg.

Place in an icing bag with a large star-shaped nozzle.

Grease a baking tray with oil and squeeze small rosettes on to it.

Brown in an oven for 10–12 minutes at 200°C (400°F/Gas Mark 6).

Serves 4
736 calories per serving
Recommended salad: 2

Dumplings

*Potatoes are ideal for making
dumplings. You must be patient,
since the round potato balls do
not always come out perfectly at
the first attempt. They may be as
hard as tennis balls, or they may
fall apart as they cook. You need
to have taken a course in body-
building to prepare dumplings
using raw potatoes, while
kneading the dough for boiled
dumplings requires the lightest of
touches. Even then, the result will
be only as good as the basic
ingredient: floury potatoes. The
first step is to find potatoes of the
right fluffy texture. Then have
confidence in your own skill and
in the tried and tested recipes on
the following pages.*

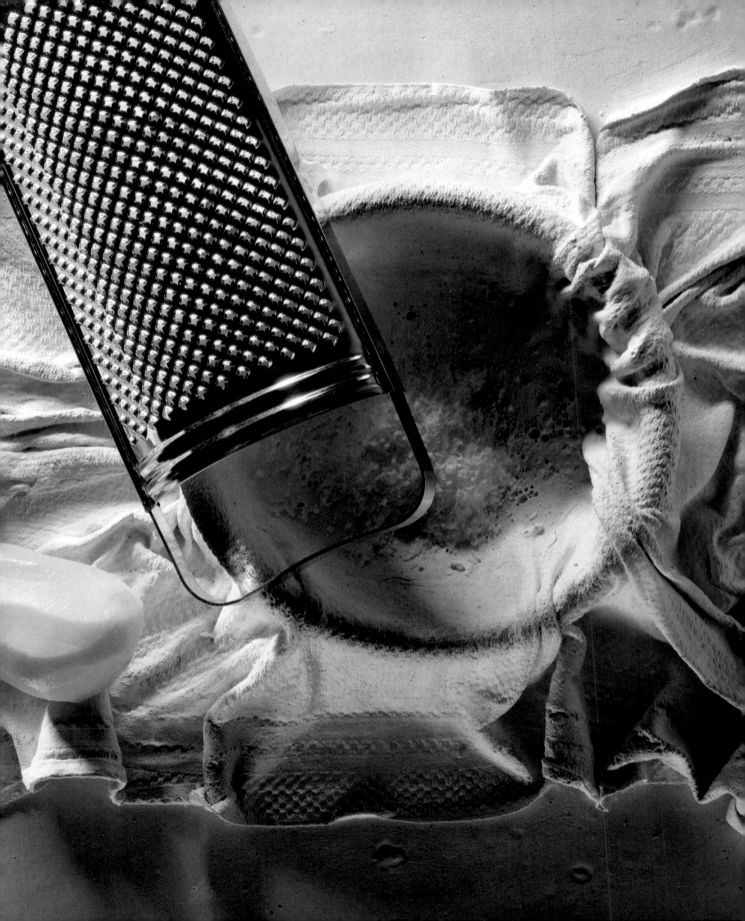

The Perfect Dumplings

5 slices white bread, crusts removed

4 tbsp oil

1.25 kg (3 lb) large, floury, preferably 'old' potatoes

115 ml (4 fl oz) milk

50 g (2 oz) semolina

200 g (7 oz) plain flour

1–2 tsp salt

nutmeg

Dice the bread. Heat the oil in a frying-pan and fry until golden brown.

Peel the potatoes and grate, using the serrated side of the grater.

Wrap the grated potatoes in a cloth and squeeze out thoroughly.

Place the potatoes in water, drain and then wring out again (they must be very dry).

Bring the milk and semolina to the boil, then stir in the potatoes.

Add the flour and beat vigorously, then knead to a dough.

Season with salt and nutmeg.

With wet hands, shape the dough into large round dumplings. Add about 3 bread dice to each dumpling and place in a saucepan with boiling salted water.

Reduce the heat and cook the dumplings in gently bubbling water for about 40 minutes.

Serves 4
572 calories per serving

Breast of Goose with Red Cabbage

2 medium-sized goose breasts

salt

freshly ground pepper

120 g (4 oz) butter

2 tbsp oil

1 finely chopped duck carcass, if available

1 bunch soup vegetables, such as leek, carrot and celery, finely chopped

3 tbsp plain flour

225 ml (8 fl oz) red wine

225 ml (8 fl oz) water, or chicken stock if duck carcass not used

10 white peppercorns

1 tbsp crème fraîche

1 tbsp dripping

1 Spanish onion, finely chopped

530 g (19 oz) canned red cabbage

115 ml (4 fl oz) cider

1 russet apple

1 tbsp apple jelly

Season the goose breasts with salt and pepper.

Heat 20 g (¾ oz) of the butter and the oil in a roasting pan, and fry the goose breasts until golden brown. Put the remaining butter in the refrigerator.

Add the carcass and chopped vegetables, and brown briefly.

Preheat the oven to 200°C (400°F/Gas Mark 6), and roast the goose breasts and vegetables in the oven for 20–30 minutes, basting frequently with the pan juices.

Remove the goose from the pan, wrap in aluminium foil and keep warm.

Sprinkle the carcass and vegetables with flour, pour in the wine and water or stock, then add the peppercorns.

Reduce the liquid by half over a high heat.

Strain the sauce through a sieve, then simmer for a further 5 minutes. In the meantime, take the butter out of the refrigerator and cut it into pieces.

Using a whisk, beat the butter into the sauce, then season to taste with salt and pepper.

Stir in the crème fraîche.

Heat the dripping in a saucepan, and sauté the onions in it.

Add the red cabbage, stir thoroughly and pour in the cider.

Cook over a low heat for 10 minutes.

Core and quarter the apple, then cut it into thin wedges.

Add to the red cabbage and cook for a further 20 minutes, until tender.

Season with apple jelly, salt and pepper.

Serve the goose with the red cabbage and sauce.

Serve with Perfect Dumplings

Serves 4
463 calories per serving

Fillets of Sole

12 fillets of sole
15 g (½ oz) butter
2 shallots, finely chopped
salt
freshly ground pepper
115 ml (4 fl oz) white wine
200 g (7 oz) crème fraîche
100 g (3 ½ oz) freshly grated horseradish
115 g (4 oz) cooked, peeled prawns
small bunch sorrel, finely chopped

Flatten the sole fillets with a knife, then roll them up.

Grease a saucepan with the butter, add the shallots and season with salt and pepper.

Add the rolled fish fillets and pour in the wine. Place the lid on the saucepan, bring to the boil, then cook over a low heat for about 2 minutes.

Remove the fish from the pan and keep warm.

Strain the stock.

Over a high heat, reduce the liquid by one-third. Add the crème fraîche and reduce by three-quarters.

Stir the horseradish into the sauce. Add the rolled fish fillets and prawns and gently heat through for about a minute, then add the sorrel.

Serve the fish with sauce and Soufflé Dumplings.

Serves 4
380 calories per serving

Soufflé Dumplings

750 g (1 ⅔ lb) floury potatoes,
    boiled in their skins
1 egg yolk
100 ml (3 ½ fl oz) double cream, whipped
6 tbsp plain flour
3 egg whites, stiffly beaten
salt
nutmeg

Boil the potatoes, then peel and allow to cool.

Rub through a sieve, then stir in the egg yolk and cream.

Stir in the flour.

Carefully fold in half the beaten egg white, then gradually add the rest. Season with salt and nutmeg.

Take soup-spoonfuls of dough and place them in boiling salted water and simmer over a low heat for about 20 minutes.

Apricot Dumplings with Poppy Seeds

1 kg (2 ¼ lb) floury potatoes, boiled in
  their skins

1–2 eggs

150 g (5 oz) plain flour

8 apricots

8 cubes sugar

55 g (2 oz) butter

3 tbsp poppy seeds

2 tbsp granulated sugar

½ tbsp ground cinnamon

Peel the boiled potatoes while still warm, then mash until smooth.

Add the eggs, stirring vigorously.

Stir in the flour.

Stone the apricots, cutting larger ones in half.

Shape the dough into dumplings the size of a tennis ball, press 1 apricot and a cube of sugar into each dumpling.

Mould the dumplings to a nice round shape, then place in lightly salted, boiling water and simmer over a low heat for about 20 minutes.

Melt the butter in a small saucepan, then stir in the poppy seeds and granulated sugar.

Remove the dumplings from the water, and drain briefly.

Sprinkle with cinnamon and pour over the poppy-seed sauce.

Serves 4
539 calories per serving

Cinnamon Dumplings

600 g (1 ¼ lb) floury potatoes

15 g (½ oz) butter

570 ml (1 pt) milk

100 g (3 ½ oz) sugar

1 tbsp cinnamon

125 g (4 ½ oz) semolina

2 eggs

butter for frying

Peel the potatoes, cut into large chunks and boil in salted water for about 20 minutes.

Drain in a sieve and allow to cool for 1–2 minutes. Rub through the sieve, then stir in the butter.

Bring the milk to the boil with the sugar and cinnamon, then slowly trickle the semolina into the saucepan.

Remove from the heat, beat in the eggs, and stir thoroughly.

While still hot, add the semolina mixture to the potatoes, mix together thoroughly and leave to cool.

Gently melt the butter in a frying-pan.

Take soup-spoonfuls of dough and slide them into the hot butter. Fry until golden brown all over.

Serve with the Fruit Compote.

Fruit Compote

3 canned or bottled pears

1 papaya

115 ml (4 fl oz) syrup from the pears

16 canned or bottled crab apples, or, if unavailable, canned or bottled lychees or kumquats

2 tsp Cointreau

1 orange

½ tsp cinnamon

100 g (3 ½ oz) butter, chilled and flaked.

Slice the pears. Peel the papaya, then cut into balls with a melon baller.

Pour the pear syrup into a saucepan and lightly warm the preserved crab apples, pears and papaya in it. Remove the fruit from the pan. Add the Cointreau to the syrup and reduce the liquid by two-thirds.

Wash the orange, and cut the rind into julienne strips. Add the rind and cinnamon to the syrup.

Stir the butter into the syrup.

Return the fruit to the pan and gently warm through.

Fillet of Venison

2 tbsp oil

450–500 g (1 lb) chopped venison bones

1 bunch soup vegetables, such as leek, carrot and celery , finely chopped

225 ml (8 fl oz) white wine

225 ml (8 fl oz) water

225 ml (8 fl oz) freshly squeezed orange juice

4 oranges

150 g (5 oz) butter, straight from the refrigerator, cut into small pieces

750 g (1 ⅔ lb) boned saddle of venison

50 g (2 oz) butter

salt

freshly ground pepper

Heat 1 tablespoon of the oil in a saucepan, and brown the venison bones and soup vegetables.

Pour in the wine and water, and reduce the liquid by half over a medium heat.

Rub through a sieve, then reduce the stock by one-quarter over a low heat.

Add the orange juice and again reduce by half.

Wash 1 orange, cut the peel into julienne strips, add to the sauce and simmer for 1–2 minutes.

Peel the other 3 oranges, remove the pith and cut all 4 oranges into thin segments.

Stir the chilled butter into the sauce, season with salt and pepper, and add some of the orange segments.

Season the venison with salt and pepper.

Heat 50 g (2 oz) butter and the remaining oil in a roasting pan and brown the meat all over. Roast in the oven at 200˚C (400˚F/Gas Mark 6) for 8–10 minutes, turning frequently.

Remove the meat from the oven, wrap in aluminium foil and leave to stand for 5 minutes.

Slice the meat, decorate with orange segments, and serve with the sauce and Mushroom Dumplings.

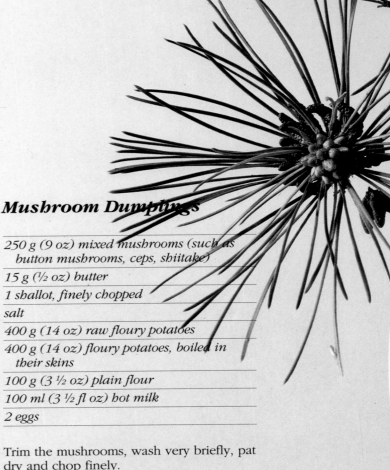

Mushroom Dumplings

250 g (9 oz) mixed mushrooms (such as button mushrooms, ceps, shiitake)

15 g (½ oz) butter

1 shallot, finely chopped

salt

400 g (14 oz) raw floury potatoes

400 g (14 oz) floury potatoes, boiled in their skins

100 g (3 ½ oz) plain flour

100 ml (3 ½ fl oz) hot milk

2 eggs

Trim the mushrooms, wash very briefly, pat dry and chop finely.

Heat the butter in a frying-pan, sauté the shallot, then add the mushrooms.

Fry for about 3 minutes until transparent, then season with salt.

Peel and grate the raw potatoes.

Wrap the grated potatoes in a cloth and squeeze thoroughly.

Peel and grate the cooked potatoes and mix with the raw potatoes.

Add the flour and stir thoroughly.

Stir in the milk.

Add the eggs and continue to stir.

Mix in the chopped mushrooms.

With wet hands, shape the dough into eight dumplings. Place in a saucepan of boiling water, reduce the heat and simmer for about 20–25 minutes.

Serves 4
507 calories per serving
Recommended salad: 4

100

Gnocchi

For fans of Italian food, potato dumplings should be on the smaller side – preferably in the form of gnocchi. These are made from the same basic ingredients, although there are also gnocchi using semolina or flour. The shape of the gnocchi is important: use your thumb to make a nice deep hollow in the middle of each potato roll. This enables the gnocchi on the plate to soak up lots of sauce or sage butter. If you like your gnocchi saucier still, press the back of a fork into the dough, creating more grooves and making the gnocchi more absorbent.

Gnocchi with Tomato Sauce and Parmesan Cheese

1 kg (2 ¼ lb) floury potatoes, boiled in their skins
2 eggs
150–250 g (5–9 oz) plain flour
salt
8 tbsp olive oil
1 onion, finely chopped
4 cloves of garlic, finely chopped
850 g (1 ¾–2 lb) canned tomatoes
1 sprig basil
100 g (3 ½ oz) Parmesan cheese, freshly grated
leaves from 1 bunch of basil
freshly ground pepper
sugar

Peel the boiled potatoes while still warm, then mash them until smooth.

Add the eggs and mix thoroughly.

Knead in enough flour to make a firm, workable dough.

Season with salt.

Roll out the potato dough on a floured wooden board until it is the thickness of a finger. Cut into pieces 1 cm (½ in) wide and 5 cm (2 in) long.

Roll the pieces into little sausage shapes. Using your thumb, press a hollow in each shape.

Place the gnocchi in a pan of boiling water and simmer over a low heat for 4–6 minutes, then drain through a sieve.

Heat 5 tablespoons of the olive oil in a saucepan, and sauté the onions and garlic in it.

Add the tomatoes and sprig of basil, and simmer for about 30 minutes.

Stir occasionally with a whisk to break up the tomatoes.

Season with salt, pepper and sugar.

Grease a warmed serving bowl with the remaining olive oil and add the gnocchi.

Pour on the tomato sauce and sprinkle with Parmesan cheese.

Sprinkle with basil and serve.

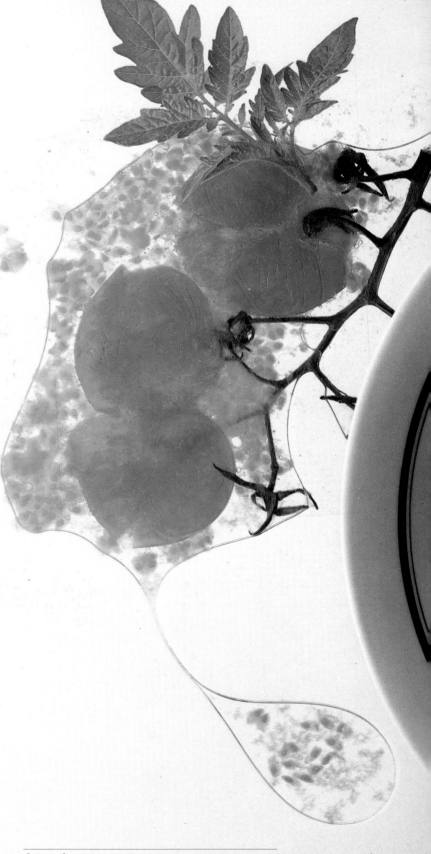

Serves 4
554 calories per serving

Spinach Gnocchi and Ricotta Cheese Bake

1 kg (2 ¼ lb) floury potatoes, boiled in
  their skins

2 eggs

200 g (7 oz) butter

3 cloves garlic, finely chopped

750 g (1 ⅔ lb) washed and trimmed
  spinach

200–300 g (7–10 oz) plain flour

salt

300 g (10 oz) ricotta cheese

Peel the boiled potatoes while still warm,
then mash them until smooth.

Add the eggs and mix thoroughly.

Heat half the butter in a large saucepan,
sauté the garlic, then add half the spinach
and cook for 3 minutes.

Finely chop or purée the rest of the
spinach and stir into the mashed potatoes.

Knead in enough flour to make a firm,
workable dough.

Season with salt.

Roll out the potato dough on a floured
wooden board until it is as thick as a
finger. Cut into pieces 1 cm (½ in) wide
and 5 cm (2 in) long.

Roll the pieces into little sausage shapes.
Using your thumb, press a hollow in each
shape.

Transfer the gnocchi to a saucepan of
boiling water and simmer over a low heat
for 4–6 minutes, then drain through a sieve.

Place the gnocchi in an ovenproof dish, stir
in the rest of the spinach and crumble the
ricotta cheese over the top.

Melt the remaining butter and pour over
the gnocchi.

Bake in the oven at 200°C (400°F/Gas
Mark 6) for 5–8 minutes until the cheese
melts.

Serves 4
1121 calories per serving

Fritters and Crêpes

Potato Fritters

1 kg (2 ¼ lb) waxy potatoes

3 spring onions

1 egg

2 tbsp plain flour

salt

oil for frying

Wash, peel and finely grate the potatoes.

Cut the white and pale green parts of the spring onions into thin rings.

Stir the egg and flour into the grated potatoes. Season with salt, and fold in the spring onions.

Heat the oil in a frying-pan.

Take soup-spoonfuls of the mixture and carefully slide them into the hot oil, flattening them slightly. Fry until a light golden brown on both sides.

Serves 4
240 calories per serving

Herb Potato Fritters

700 g (1 ½ lb) floury potatoes

15 g (½ oz) butter

1 egg

3 tbsp plain flour

small bunch parsley, finely chopped

small bunch basil, finely chopped

salt

freshly ground pepper

oil for frying

Peel the potatoes and cut into chunks. Cook in salted water for about 20 minutes, then drain in a sieve. Rub them through the sieve while still warm.

Stir in the butter. Add the egg, flour, parsley and basil, and stir thoroughly. Season with salt and pepper.

Heat the oil in a frying-pan and cook as above.

Serves 4
173 calories per serving

109

Quail Breasts

4 quail

salt

2 tbsp oil

1 sprig rosemary

115 ml (4 fl oz) apple juice

115 ml (4 fl oz) white wine

3 tbsp honey

50 g (2 oz) butter, straight from the
   refrigerator and cut into small pieces

freshly ground pepper

4 courgette flowers

Season the quail with salt.

Heat the oil in a heat-proof casserole, and
brown the quail all over.

Transfer the quail to the oven and cook at
200°C (400°F/Gas Mark 6) for 10 minutes.

Remove the quail from the oven, wrap in
aluminium foil and keep warm.

Pour off the fat, reheat the casserole and
sauté the rosemary.

Add the apple juice, bring to the boil, then
pour in the wine.

Reduce the liquid by half, stir in the honey
and return to the boil.

Stir the butter into the sauce.

Discard the rosemary and season the sauce
with salt and pepper.

Add the courgette flowers and simmer for a
further 4 minutes.

Unwrap the quail breasts and serve with
the courgette flowers, sauce and Herb
Potato Fritters.

Serves 4
288 calories per serving

110

Langoustine in Mushroom Sauce with Potato Fritters

25 g (1 oz) butter

1 onion, finely chopped

250–400 g (8–14 oz) mixed mushrooms (such as shiitake, button mushrooms, oyster mushrooms)

100 g (3 ½ oz) crème fraîche

1 cooked langoustine

leaves of 1 bunch basil, cut into strips

salt

freshly ground pepper

Heat the butter in a frying-pan and sauté the onion.

Clean the mushrooms, discarding the stalks if you prefer, and add to the onions.

When the mushrooms are glazed, add the crème fraîche and simmer gently for 5 minutes.

Break the langoustine into pieces and cut the tail into not-too-thick slices. Add to the mushroom sauce and heat through gently.

Season to taste with salt and pepper.

Sprinkle with basil and serve with Potato Fritters.

Serves 4
112 calories per serving

Potato Blinis

250 g (9 oz) plain flour

20 g (¾ oz) yeast

1 tsp sugar

115 ml (4 fl oz) lukewarm milk

200 g (7 oz) floury potatoes

1 tsp salt

1 egg

50 g (2 oz) butter, melted

fat for frying

Sift the flour into a bowl.

Dissolve the yeast and sugar in some of the milk.

Make a well in the sifted flour and pour in the yeast mixture.

Cover the yeast mixture with flour, then leave to prove in a warm place for 20 minutes.

Wash and peel the potatoes, then boil in salted water for about 20 minutes.

Drain in a sieve, allow to cool a little, then rub through the sieve.

Add the salt to the flour and knead to a dough.

Stir the egg and butter into the mashed potatoes. Add the potatoes to the dough and knead thoroughly.

Leave the dough to prove for a further 20 minutes.

Heat the fat in a frying-pan. Take soup-spoonfuls of dough and carefully slide them into the hot fat, flattening them slightly.

Fry until the blinis are a light golden brown on both sides.

Serves 4
797 calories per serving

Smoked Salmon with Caviare and Quail Eggs

8 quail eggs

200 g (7 oz) crème fraîche

2 limes (slice ½ lime, and squeeze the juice from the rest)

salt

freshly ground pepper

small bunch dill, finely chopped

400 g (14 oz) thinly sliced smoked salmon

50 g (2 oz) caviare

leaves from 2 stems of dill

Boil the quail eggs for 4 minutes, rinse in cold water, and shell.

Mix the crème fraîche with the lime juice, salt, pepper and dill, adjusting the seasoning as necessary.

Arrange the Potato Blinis on individual plates, and spread with crème fraîche.

Arrange the smoked salmon, caviare, quail eggs and lime slices on and around the blinis. Serve sprinkled with dill.

Fruit-Filled Crêpes

250 g (8 oz) potatoes

4 eggs

125 g (4 ½) oz plain flour

115–225 ml (4–8 fl oz) milk

salt

a little oil

fruit filling (see opposite)

icing sugar

Peel, boil and mash the potatoes.

Mix the eggs into the potatoes.

Sieve the flour into the mixture and stir.

Stir in enough milk to make a runny batter.

Add a pinch of salt and leave for 10 minutes.

Heat a little oil in a frying-pan.

Ladle the batter into the pan and spread very thinly and evenly.

Fry until bubbles form on the surface and the edges look dry, then turn and cook the other side until golden brown.

Slide on to a plate, cover half the crêpe with fruit filling and fold over the other half.

Sprinkle with icing sugar and serve.

Serves 4
295 calories per serving

1

1 small melon
1 papaya
2 tbsp Grand Marnier
1 tbsp icing sugar

Peel the melon and make into balls with a melon baller. Peel the papaya and cut into pieces.

Mix the two with Grand Marnier and icing sugar, and leave for 30 minutes.

2

200 g (7 oz) raspberries
200 g (7 oz) blackberries
2 tbsp kirsch
2 tbsp icing sugar

Mix the berries with the kirsch and the icing sugar, and leave for 30 minutes.

3

250 g (8 oz) strawberries
1 tbsp icing sugar
225 ml (8 fl oz) double cream
1 tbsp granulated sugar

Slice the strawberries, mix with the icing sugar and leave for 30 minutes. Beat the cream until stiff and sugar to taste. Combine the strawberries and cream.

4

2 oranges
115 ml (4 fl oz) port
50 g (2 oz) granulated sugar
4 figs

Wash one of the oranges and finely grate the peel. Peel both oranges, separate into segments and remove the pips.

Place the grated peel and segments in a saucepan with the port and sugar, and bring to the boil.

Reduce heat, add the figs and simmer for 10 minutes until soft.

115

Potato Waffles

250 g (9 oz) waxy potatoes
250 g (9 oz) plain flour
150 g (5 oz) icing sugar
225 ml (8 fl oz) milk
50 g (2 oz) coconut flakes
3 egg whites, stiffly beaten
oil for greasing

Wash and peel the potatoes, then cut into chunks.

Boil in lightly salted water for about 15 minutes.

Drain in a colander and leave to cool a little.

Mash the potatoes and sift the flour on top.

Add the icing sugar and milk and stir to a smooth batter.

Stir in the coconut flakes.

Carefully fold in the egg whites.

Heat the waffle iron and brush lightly with oil.

Using a small ladle, pour the batter into the waffle iron and cook until the waffles are a light golden brown.

Serve with blackcurrant ice cream and Redcurrant Compote or lemon ice cream and Apple Compote.

Serves 4
502 calories per serving

116

Redcurrant Compote

500 g (18 oz) redcurrants, stalks removed

225 ml (8 fl oz) redcurrant juice

4 tbsp sugar

Bring the redcurrants to the boil with the juice and sugar and continue to cook for about 2 minutes.

Apple Compote

450 g (1 lb) tart apples

juice of 1 lemon

100 ml (3 ½ fl oz) water

80 g (3 oz) sugar

1 cinnamon stick

Peel and core the apples, and cut into quarters.

Place in a saucepan, and add the lemon juice, water, sugar and cinnamon.

Place the lid on the pan, bring to the boil, then simmer over a low heat for about 10 minutes.

Discard the cinnamon stick before serving.

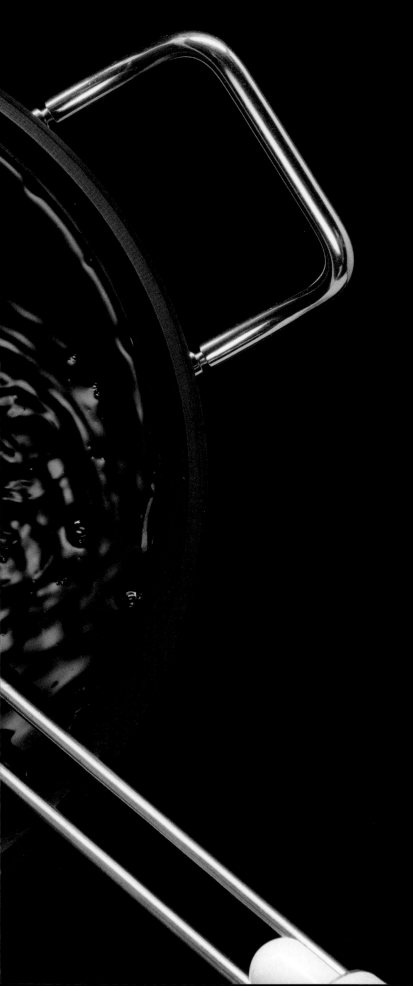

Deep-Fried Potatoes

You buy a bag of golden chips from a shop. They are still a bit too hot but you cannot wait to tuck in – it's an experience we have all shared. However, real gourmets fry their own. They can be sure the fat is really fresh, making the chips taste even better.

Deep-frying is quite easy. All you need is hot vegetable oil – and plenty of it! First heat it in a chip pan or deep-fryer to at least 180°C (350°F). If you do not have a kitchen thermometer, you can test the oil with a wooden spoon. The fat is hot enough when little bubbles rise from the spoon. Then add the chips, croquettes or potato balls (you will find the recipes on the following pages).

To avoid the fat cooling down too much, it is best to fry only a small batch of potatoes at a time. Take the potatoes out of the oil after a few minutes – as soon as the outsides are crisp and golden. Drain them briefly on kitchen towels, then serve piping hot.

Champion Chips and French Fries

1 kg (2 ¼ lb) floury potatoes

oil for deep-frying

salt

Wash and peel the potatoes.

First slice the potatoes, then cut them into large chips or thinner sticks for french fries.

Rinse, drain in a colander, and pat thoroughly dry with kitchen towels.

Heat the oil to 120˚C (250˚F), and blanch the potatoes in batches for 3 minutes each.

Remove the potatoes from the pan and drain on kitchen towels.

Meanwhile, reheat the oil to 180˚C (350˚F), then return the potatoes to the pan and fry until crisp and golden.

Drain on kitchen towels and serve sprinkled with salt.

You can also use frozen chips or french fries, in which case follow the instructions on the packet.

Serves 4
500 calories per serving

Pepper Steak

4 fillet steaks,
each weighing 200 g (7 oz)

3 tbsp oil

15 g (½ oz) butter

salt

115 ml (4 fl oz) white wine

225 ml (8 fl oz) single cream

2 tbsp green peppercorns

freshly ground pepper

Heat the oil in a frying-pan and sear the
steaks over a high heat.

Turn down the heat, add the butter and fry
the steaks for 10–15 minutes, turning
several times.

Remove the steaks from the pan, season
with salt on both sides, wrap in aluminium
foil and keep warm.

Pour off the excess fat in the pan. Pour the
wine into the remaining juices.

Reduce the liquid by half, then add the
cream and reduce by one-third.

Add the green peppercorns to the sauce
and season to taste with salt and pepper.
Pour the sauce over the steaks, and serve
with Champion Chips or French Fries.

Serves 4
525 calories per serving
Recommended salad: 3

122

Chicken in Mushroom Sauce

1 roasting chicken

salt

freshly ground pepper

2 tbsp oil

15 g (½ oz) butter

1 onion, finely chopped

115 ml (4 fl oz) white wine

225 ml (8 fl oz) single cream

150 g (5 oz) button mushrooms

a little lemon juice

Divide the chicken into 8 joints and season with salt and pepper.

Heat the oil and butter in a saucepan, and fry the chicken joints until brown all over.

Pour off the excess fat, then add the onion, and sauté.

Add the wine, bring to the boil, then reduce slightly.

Add the cream and gently simmer over a low heat for 30 minutes.

Clean and finely slice the mushrooms.

Add the mushrooms to the pan 10 minutes before the end of the cooking time.

Season to taste with salt, pepper and lemon juice.

Serve with Champion Chips or French Fries.

Serves 4

353 calories per serving

Croquette Potatoes

500 g (18 oz) floury potatoes
2 egg yolks
salt
nutmeg
2 tbsp finely chopped parsley
flour for coating
1 beaten egg
breadcrumbs for coating
oil for deep-frying

Peel the potatoes and cook them in boiling salted water for about 20 minutes.

Drain in a colander, allow to cool a little, then, while still hot, mash until smooth.

Stir in the egg yolks, and season with salt and nutmeg.

Mix the chopped parsley into the potatoes, them shape into small, thick rolls.

Coat the croquettes first in flour, then in beaten egg and finally in breadcrumbs.

Fry in oil at 180˚C (350˚F) for 5 minutes until golden.

Serves 4
350 calories per serving

Rabbit in Mustard Sauce

4 rabbit forelegs

salt

freshly ground pepper

2 tbsp oil

115 ml (4 fl oz) white wine

150 g (5 oz) crème fraîche

3 tbsp coarse-grained mustard

1 bunch tarragon, finely chopped

1 bunch spring carrots

25 g (1 oz) butter

300 g (10 oz) canned chestnuts

150 g (5 oz) honey

Season the rabbit with salt and pepper.

Heat the oil in a saucepan, and fry the rabbit until browned all over.

Roast in the oven at 200°C (400°F/Gas Mark 6) for 20 minutes, then wrap in aluminium foil and leave to stand.

Pour off the excess fat from the pan.

Add the wine to the remaining juices, then add the crème fraîche and simmer for 5 minutes.

Season with salt, pepper and mustard.

Add the tarragon, but do not return to the boil.

Scrape the carrots and cook in salted water until tender but still crisp.

Melt the butter and toss the carrots in it.

Heat the chestnuts through with the juice from the can and the honey.

Serve the rabbit with the sauce, carrots, chestnuts and Potato Croquettes.

Serves 4
574 calories per serving
Recommended salad: 2

Almond Potato Balls

1 kg (2 ¼ lb) floury potatoes

1 egg yolk

salt

flour for coating

1 beaten egg

breadcrumbs for coating

100 g (3 ½ oz) flaked almonds

oil for deep-frying

Wash and peel the potatoes, then cut them into chunks.

Boil in salted water for about 20 minutes, drain in a colander and allow to cool a little.

Mash the potatoes until smooth, stir in the egg yolk and season with salt.

Shape into small balls, and coat them first in flour, next in beaten egg, then in breadcrumbs and finally in almond flakes.

Fry in oil at about 170°C (325°F) for about 4 minutes until golden brown.

Serves 4
306 calories per serving

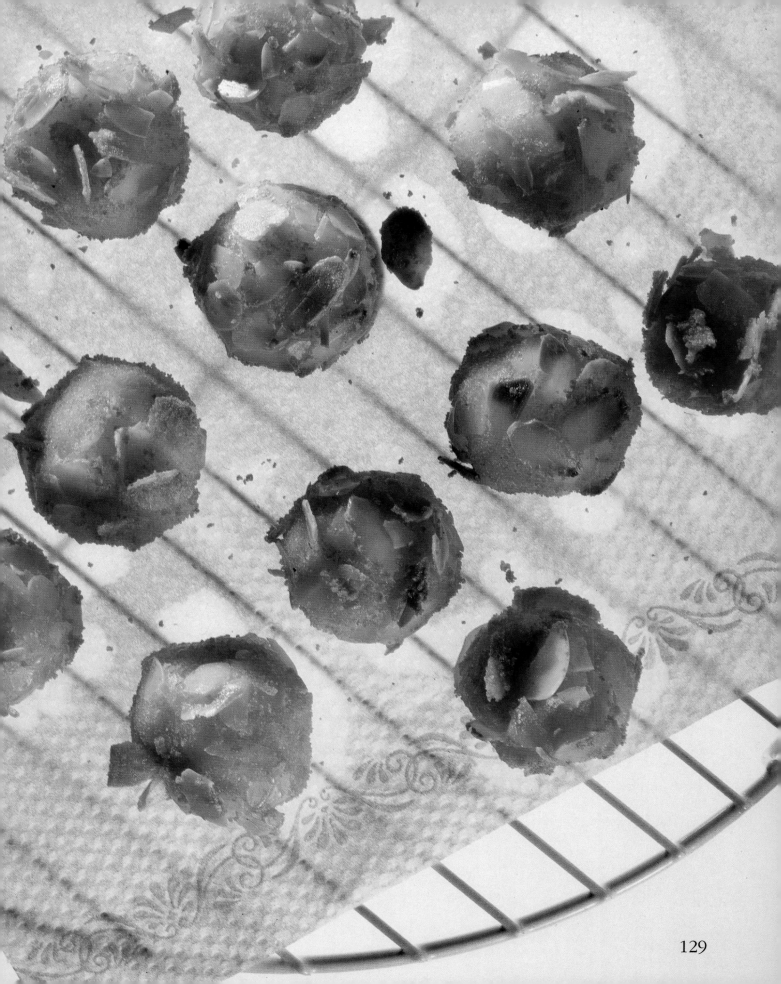

Breast of Pheasant with Figs and Pepper Sauce

4 pheasant breasts
salt
freshly ground pepper
1 pig's caul (order from the butcher) or thin slices of unsmoked streaky bacon
1 tbsp oil
15 g (½ oz) butter
2 sweet red peppers
225 ml (8 fl oz) single cream
225 g (8 oz) canned figs in syrup

Season the pheasant breasts with salt and pepper.

Arrange each pair of breasts with the fleshy sides towards each other and wrap in half the caul and secure tightly. If you cannot obtain a caul, use very thin slices of unsmoked streaky bacon.

Heat the oil and butter in a heat-proof casserole, and brown the pheasant breasts all over.

Roast in the oven at 200°C (400°F/Gas Mark 6) for 15–20 minutes, basting frequently with the pan juices.

Remove the meat from the oven, wrap in aluminium foil and keep warm.

Grill the peppers until blisters form on the skins. Remove from the grill and peel while still hot.

Coarsely chop 1 ½ peppers, and cut the remaining half into diamond shapes.

Pour the cream into a saucepan, add the chopped peppers and bring to the boil, then simmer for 5 minutes.

Purée in a blender and season with salt and pepper.

Add the pepper diamonds to the sauce.

In another saucepan briefly warm the figs in their syrup.

Carve the pheasant breasts diagonally into slices.

Serve with the sauce, figs and Almond Potato Balls.

Serves 4
400 calories per serving

Venison in Gingerbread Sauce

2 tbsp oil

800 g (1 ¾ lb) haunch of venison

salt

freshly ground pepper

225 ml (8 fl oz) red wine

225 ml (8 fl oz) game stock

3 slices gingerbread cake

1 tbsp cornflour

100 g (3 ½ oz) butter, straight from the refrigerator, cut into small pieces

250 g (9 oz) oyster mushrooms

15 g (½ oz) butter

1 bunch parsley, finely chopped

250 g (9 oz) preserved gooseberries

50 g (2 oz) sugar

juice of 1 lemon

2 tbsp water

Heat the oil in a large, heat-proof casserole and brown the venison all over.

Season with salt and pepper, then roast in the oven at 200°C (400°F/Gas Mark 6) for 20 minutes.

Pour the wine over the meat and cook for a further 20–30 minutes, basting frequently.

Remove the meat from the oven, wrap in aluminium foil and keep warm.

Add the stock to the pan juices, crumble in the gingerbread, then reduce the sauce by half. Strain the sauce through a sieve, then bind with cornflour.

Stir the chilled butter into the sauce.

Clean the oyster mushrooms, discarding the tough stalks.

Heat 15 g (½ oz) butter in a frying-pan and sauté the mushrooms.

Season with salt and pepper, and sprinkle with parsley.

Place the gooseberries in a saucepan with sugar, lemon juice and water, and bring briefly to the boil.

Carve the venison into thin slices and arrange on individual plates.

Serve with sauce, oyster mushrooms, gooseberries and Potato Pears.

Potato Pears

1 kg (2 ¼ lb) floury potatoes

1 egg

flour for coating

1 beaten egg

breadcrumbs for coating

salt

freshly ground pepper

cloves

Wash and peel the potatoes and cut them into chunks.

Cook in salted water for about 20 minutes, then drain in a colander and leave to cool.

Mash the potatoes until smooth, stir in the egg, and season with salt and pepper.

With wet hands, form the mashed potatoes into small pear shapes.

Coat the potato pears first in flour, then in beaten egg and finally in breadcrumbs.

Deep-fry in oil at a temperature of 180°C (350°F) for about 5 minutes until they are a light golden brown, then drain on kitchen towels.

Garnish each pear, using a clove as the 'flower' and a parsley stem as the 'stalk'.

Serves 4
724 calories per serving

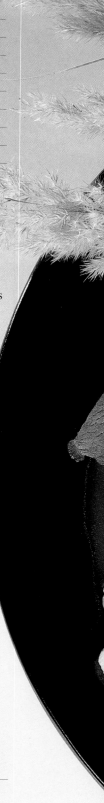

Deep-Fried Vegetables in Beer Batter

4 small beetroot

1 bunch small white turnips

1 bunch carrots

4 young leeks

250 g (9 oz) floury potatoes

200 g (7 oz) sifted flour

225 ml (8 fl oz) beer

1 tsp salt

4 egg whites, stiffly beaten

oil for deep-frying

Clean and peel the vegetables.

Cook the beetroot in boiling salted water for 20 minutes, then drain in a colander. Allow to cool completely before slicing.

Cut the leeks into diagonal pieces. Leave the turnips and carrots whole. Cook the turnips, carrots and leeks separately in boiling water, or steam, until tender but still crisp.

Drain in a colander and rinse under cold running water.

Peel the potatoes and boil in salted water for about 20 minutes. Drain in a colander and allow to cool a little, then mash until smooth.

Mix the flour, beer and salt. Add to the mashed potatoes and mix to a smooth batter.

Very carefully fold in the egg whites.

Coat the vegetables in the batter and deep-fry in oil at 180°C (350°F) for 6–7 minutes.

Options

Try cooking other vegetables, such as broccoli, baby corncobs, celery and peppers, in the same way.

Serves 4

409 calories per serving

Potato Nests

1 kg (2 ¼ lb) waxy potatoes
oil for deep-frying
salt
1 bunch young beetroot
1 bunch small white turnips
1 bunch spring carrots
85 g (3 oz) butter
1 bunch parsley, finely chopped
1 bunch basil, cut into thin strips

Peel and thinly slice the potatoes, then cut them into matchsticks. Wash and drain in a sieve, and dry thoroughly with kitchen towels.

Using a double chip basket (see photo), deep-fry in batches in oil at 180°C (350°F) for 6–7 minutes.

Drain on kitchen towels and sprinkle with salt.

Clean and peel the vegetables.

Cook the beetroot in boiling salted water for 20 minutes. Drain in a colander. Cut into quarters when cold.

Cook the turnips and carrots in boiling salted water until tender but still crisp. Drain in a colander and rinse under cold running water.

Heat one-third of the butter in a frying-pan for each vegetable, and toss the vegetables separately. Sprinkle the carrots with parsley, and the turnips with basil.

Serve the potato nests with the vegetables.

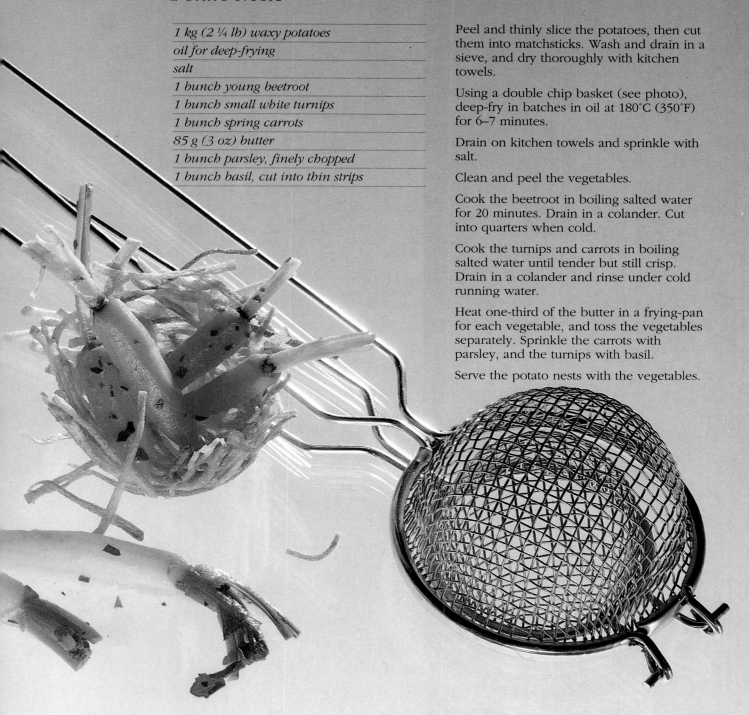

Serves 4
355 calories per serving

Gratins and Bakes

Gratin dauphinois *is one of the most aristocratic of all potato dishes. Sliced and baked in the oven, topped with cheese and served as a side dish, the recipe for potatoes 'in the style of the heir to the throne' is one of the simplest in the world.*

There are endless varieties of potato bakes. They can be served as starters in tiny dishes or provide a complete meal, packed with filling ingredients. For all their gold-encrusted splendour, they are also practical. You can prepare them in advance, then pop them in the oven when you are ready and bring them straight to the table.

Courgette and Potato Gratin

250 g (9 oz) waxy potatoes, boiled in their skins

250 g (9 oz) courgettes

65 g (2 ½ oz) butter

2 garlic cloves

salt

freshly ground pepper

1 bunch tarragon, finely chopped

225 ml (8 fl oz) single cream

50 g (2 oz) Emmenthal cheese, grated

Peel and slice the potatoes while they are still warm.

Wash and slice the courgettes.

Grease a baking dish with about 15 g (½ oz) of butter, and arrange the potatoes and courgettes in alternating, overlapping layers. Place the remaining butter in the refrigerator until needed.

Crush the garlic in a garlic press.

Stir the garlic, salt, pepper and tarragon into the cream.

Pour the cream over the vegetables, sprinkle with grated cheese and top with flakes of chilled butter. Bake in the oven at 225°C (425°F/Gas Mark 7) for 20–25 minutes until light golden brown.

Serves 4
373 calories per serving

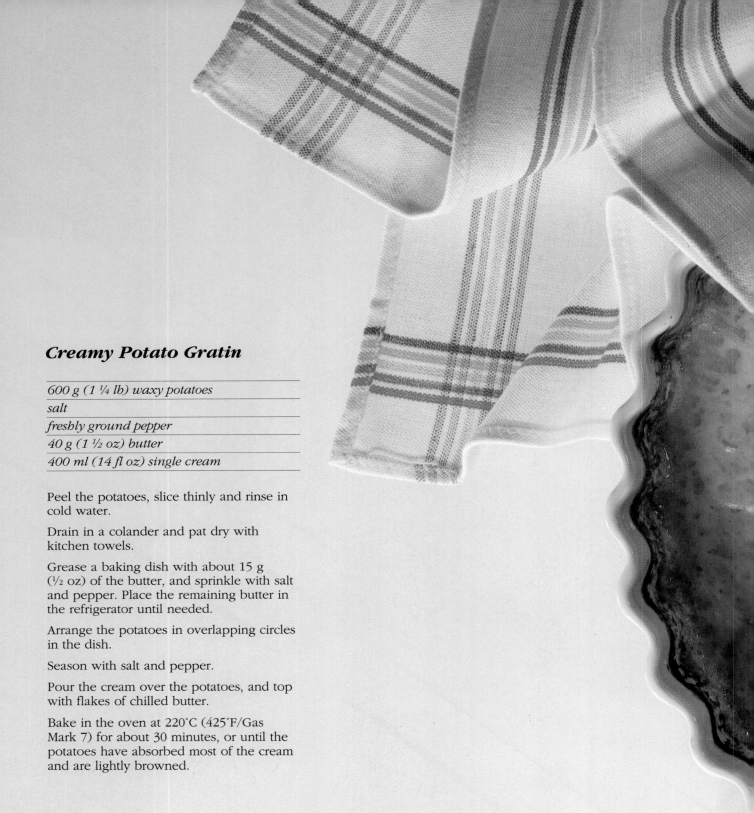

Creamy Potato Gratin

600 g (1 ¼ lb) waxy potatoes

salt

freshly ground pepper

40 g (1 ½ oz) butter

400 ml (14 fl oz) single cream

Peel the potatoes, slice thinly and rinse in cold water.

Drain in a colander and pat dry with kitchen towels.

Grease a baking dish with about 15 g (½ oz) of the butter, and sprinkle with salt and pepper. Place the remaining butter in the refrigerator until needed.

Arrange the potatoes in overlapping circles in the dish.

Season with salt and pepper.

Pour the cream over the potatoes, and top with flakes of chilled butter.

Bake in the oven at 220°C (425°F/Gas Mark 7) for about 30 minutes, or until the potatoes have absorbed most of the cream and are lightly browned.

Serves 4
434 calories per serving

Aubergine and Potato Bake

2 small aubergines (300 g/10 oz)

salt

4 tbsp olive oil

1 onion, finely chopped

1 garlic clove, finely chopped

400 g (14 oz) tomatoes

1 bunch basil

700 g (1 ½ lb) waxy potatoes

200 g (7 oz) mozzarella cheese

15 g (½ oz) butter

freshly ground pepper

Slice the aubergines, sprinkle with salt and leave to stand with a weight on top for about 30 minutes. Pat dry with kitchen towels.

Heat 3 tablespoons of oil in a frying-pan and fry the aubergines, in batches if necessary, and set aside.

Heat the remaining oil in the pan and sauté the onion and garlic.

Wash and coarsely chop the tomatoes. Add them to the garlic and onions, and simmer for 45 minutes.

Rub the tomatoes through a sieve and season with salt and pepper.

Cut the basil into thin strips and add to the sauce.

Peel and slice the potatoes.

Cook in boiling water for 5 minutes, then drain in a colander.

Drain and slice the mozzarella cheese.

Butter a baking dish, and arrange the aubergines, potatoes, mozzarella and tomato sauce in layers, finishing with tomato sauce and mozzarella.

Bake in the oven at 200°C (400°F/Gas Mark 6) for about 40 minutes.

Serves 4
313 calories per serving

Leek and Potato Gratin with Chervil

1 kg (2 ¼ lb) small new potatoes
400 g (14 oz) leeks
salt
freshly ground pepper
55 g (2 oz) butter
100 g (3 ½ oz) chervil
400 ml (14 fl oz) single cream

Wash and scrub the potatoes.

Wash the leeks. Discard the dark green parts, then cut the remainder diagonally into pieces.

Cook the leeks in boiling salted water for 1 minute, drain in a colander and rinse under cold running water.

Grease a baking dish with about 15 g (½ oz) of the butter and line with the leeks. Place the remainder of the butter in the refrigerator until needed.

Arrange the potatoes on top of the leeks, and season with salt and pepper.

Sprinkle the chervil over the potatoes, then pour in the cream.

Sprinkle the butter flakes on top, then cover the dish with aluminium foil.

Bake in the oven at 200°C (400°F/Gas Mark 6) for about 60 minutes.

Serves 4
586 calories per serving

Mixed Vegetable Gratin

1 kg (2 ¼ lb) floury potatoes

800 ml (1 ⅖ pt) milk

225 g (8 oz) butter

salt

freshly ground pepper

nutmeg

500 g (18 oz) broccoli

1 bunch carrots

2–3 small kohlrabi

2 leeks

2 tbsp plain flour

100 g (3 ½ oz) Emmenthal cheese, grated

Peel the potatoes and cook in boiling salted water for about 20 minutes. Drain in a colander and allow to cool a little. Mash until smooth while still warm.

Bring 225 ml (8 fl oz) of the milk and 100 g (3 ½ oz) of the butter to the boil together, then stir into the potatoes. Season with salt, pepper and nutmeg.

Wash and trim the vegetables, peeling if necessary. Divide the broccoli into florets. Slice the carrots and kohlrabi. Cut the leek into diagonal pieces.

Cook each vegetable separately in boiling salted water until tender but crisp, drain in a colander and rinse under cold water.

Heat 40 g (1 ½ oz) of the butter, then stir in the flour. Slowly add the remaining milk, stirring constantly to avoid lumps forming. Bring to the boil, then simmer for 15 minutes.

Stir in the cheese and season the sauce with salt and pepper.

Grease a baking dish with 15 g (½ oz) butter, arrange the vegetables in layers in the dish, and pour over the cheese sauce. Chill the remaining butter until needed.

Put the potato purée in a piping bag with a star-shaped nozzle and pipe on top of the vegetables.

Sprinkle with flakes of the chilled butter and bake in the oven at 180°C (350°F/Gas Mark 4) for 40 minutes.

Serves 4
937 calories per serving

Oven Specialities

Potatoes with Rosemary and Garlic

1 kg (2 ¼ lb) small waxy potatoes
6 tbsp olive oil
6 cloves garlic
leaves from 3 sprigs rosemary
coarse salt

Wash, scrub and halve the potatoes. Arrange them in a roasting pan and drizzle with olive oil.

Peel the garlic and cut crossways into thin slices.

Sprinkle the garlic and rosemary over the potatoes, and season with salt.

Cover the pan with greaseproof paper, and roast the potatoes in the oven at 200˚C (400˚F/Gas Mark 6) for about 20 minutes.

Remove from the oven, discard the greaseproof paper and turn the potatoes over.

Return to the oven for 25–30 minutes.

Serves 4
207 calories per serving
Recommended salad: 5

Baked Potatoes with Caviare

4 medium-sized, firm-textured potatoes

200 g (7 oz) crème fraîche

salt

freshly ground pepper

1 bunch chives, finely chopped

50 g (2 oz) caviare

Wash and scrub the potatoes. Wrap each potato in a piece of aluminium foil large enough to cover it completely.

Bake in the oven at 220°C (425°F/Gas Mark 7) for about 60 minutes.

Season the crème fraîche with salt and pepper, and stir in the chives.

Unwrap the potatoes and gently break open the tops with a fork.

Pile the crème fraîche on top, and serve sprinkled with caviare.

Serves 4
192 calories per serving

Potato Pie

500 g (18 oz) floury potatoes

350 g (12 ½ oz) plain flour

165 g (6 oz) butter

½ tsp salt

300 ml (½ pt) water

2 eggs

150 g (5 oz) Emmenthal cheese, finely diced

2 egg yolks

100 ml (3 ½ fl oz) milk

2 egg whites, stiffly beaten

Peel the potatoes and boil in salted water for about 20 minutes.

Drain in a colander and allow to cool a little.

Knead 300 g (10 ½ oz) of the flour and 150 g (5 oz) of the butter together, add salt, one-third of the water and the 2 eggs, and work to a smooth dough.

On a floured pastry board, roll out the dough into a circular piece about 29 cm (11 ½ in) in diameter.

Grease a suitably sized flan dish with about 15 g (½ oz) butter, and lay the pastry in the dish.

Mash the potatoes until smooth and stir in the cheese.

Mix the egg yolks with the remaining flour and water and the milk, then fold in the egg whites.

Carefully fold the egg mixture into the potatoes.

Fill the pastry shell with the potato and cheese mixture.

Bake in the oven at 200°C (400°F /Gas Mark 6) for 30–40 minutes, until a light golden brown.

Serves 4
932 calories per serving

154

Apple Turnovers

1 kg (2 ¼ lb) floury potatoes
150 g (5 oz) plain flour
salt
2 eggs
100 g (3 ½ oz) clarified butter, melted
500 g (18 oz) green apples
20 ml (1 fl oz) Calvados
155 g (5 ½ oz) sugar
200 g (7 oz) soured cream
flour for rolling
115 ml (4 fl oz) milk
1 tbsp ground cinnamon

Peel the potatoes and cook in boiling salted water for about 20 minutes.

Drain in a colander. Mash until smooth while still hot and leave to cool.

Add the flour, salt and eggs to the potatoes and knead to a dough. Shape the dough into a sausage, then cut into portions 6 cm (2 ½ in) long.

On a floured surface, roll each portion into a circle about 15 cm (6 in) in diameter, and brush with melted butter.

Peel and core the apples, then cut, first into quarters and then into thin slices. Sprinkle with Calvados. Leave to stand for 5 minutes, then arrange on top of the pastry circles, sprinkle with about 125 (4 ½ oz) sugar and top each turnover with 1 tablespoon soured cream.

Roll up each turnover, folding the sides in and pressing the ends down firmly. Grease a baking dish with melted butter, arrange the turnovers tightly side by side, and brush with melted butter. Bake in the oven at 200°C (400°F/Gas Mark 6) for about 40 minutes.

When the top is lightly browned, heat the milk and pour over the turnovers.

Continue to cook until all the milk has been absorbed.

Mix the remaining sugar and cinnamon, and sprinkle over the turnovers.

Serves 4
831 calories per serving

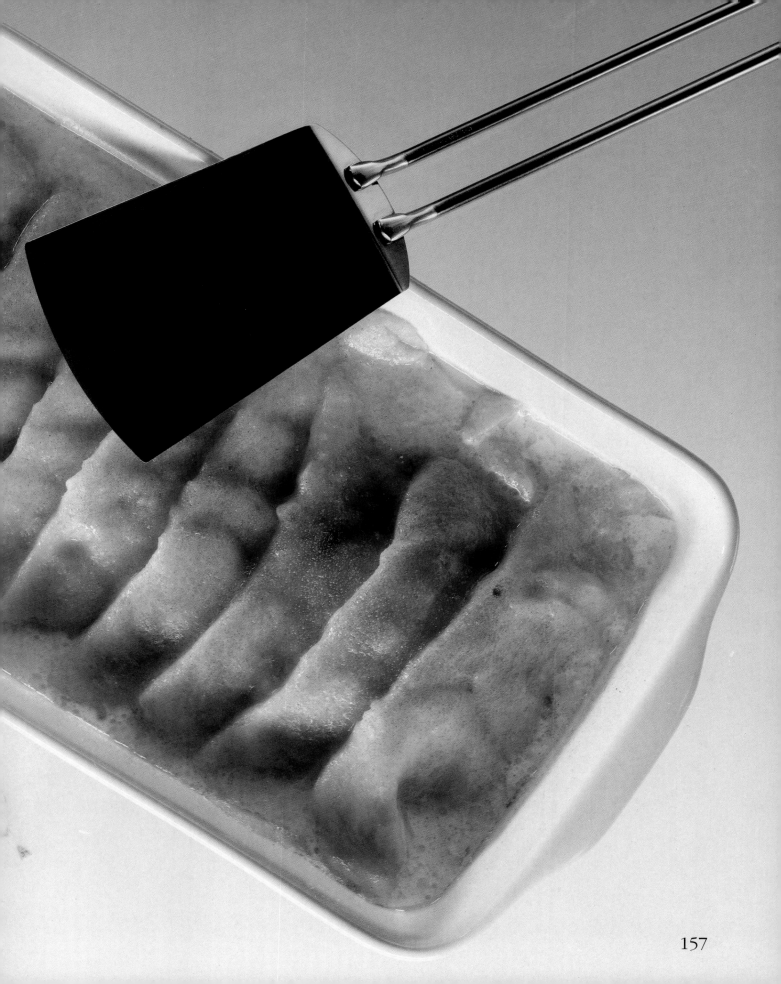

157

Potato Soufflé

750 (1 ⅔ lb) floury potatoes

100 g (3 ½ oz) butter

3 egg yolks

100 g (3 ½ oz) Emmenthal cheese,
   freshly grated

salt

nutmeg

3 egg whites, stiffly beaten

breadcrumbs for lining the dish

Peel the potatoes and cook them in salted water for about 20 minutes.

Drain in a colander and allow to cool a little.

Mash the potatoes until smooth and leave to cool a bit longer.

Stir about 60 g (2 oz) of the butter into the mashed potatoes a little at a time.

Add the egg yolks and 70 g (2 ½ oz) of the cheese, then season with salt and nutmeg.

Carefully fold in the egg whites.

Grease a soufflé dish with about 15 g (½ oz) of the butter, and line with breadcrumbs. Put the remaining butter into the refrigerator until needed.

Fill the dish three-quarters full with the potato mixture, sprinkle with the remaining cheese and top with flakes of chilled butter.

Bake in the oven at 200°C (400°F/Gas Mark 6) for about 60 minutes.

Serves 4
427 calories per serving

Bread and Cake

If you haven't tried it, you would never believe it: you can even make bread from potatoes. To amaze your friends, invite them to drop round for a snack and serve them the two loaves and the savoury pastries shown on the following pages. To enjoy them at their best, make sure you eat them fresh and still warm from the oven. Potatoes also make delicious cakes: try the recipe for Potato-Almond Cake.

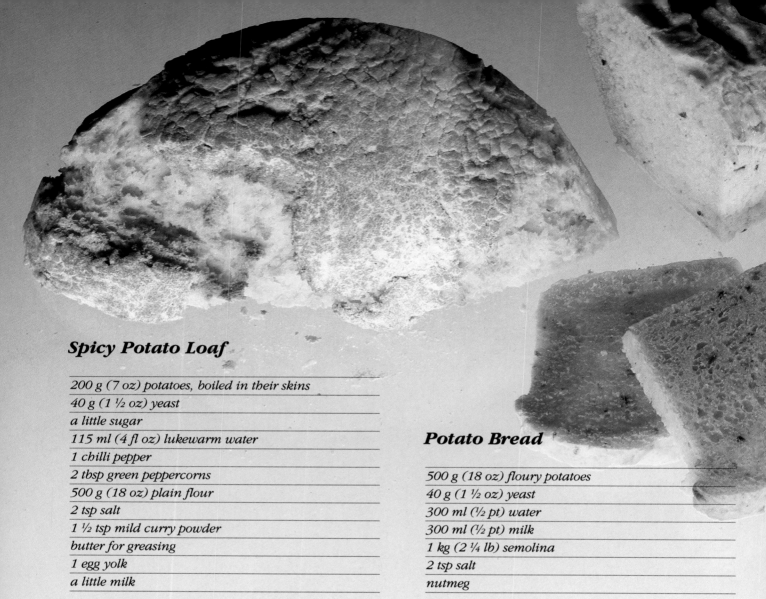

Spicy Potato Loaf

200 g (7 oz) potatoes, boiled in their skins
40 g (1 ½ oz) yeast
a little sugar
115 ml (4 fl oz) lukewarm water
1 chilli pepper
2 tbsp green peppercorns
500 g (18 oz) plain flour
2 tsp salt
1 ½ tsp mild curry powder
butter for greasing
1 egg yolk
a little milk

Peel the potatoes while still warm, and mash.

Dissolve the yeast and sugar in the lukewarm water.

Crush the chilli pepper, using a pestle and mortar. Mix the mashed potatoes with the chilli, green peppercorns, flour, salt and curry powder.

Add the yeast mixture to the flour and knead to a smooth dough, adding more water, as necessary. Cover the dough and leave to prove in a warm place for about 30 minutes. Knead thoroughly again.

Butter a loaf tin and place the dough in it.

Mix the egg yolk with milk, and use to brush the loaf. Score the top of the loaf in a diagonal pattern, then leave to prove for another 20 minutes.

Bake in the oven at 200°C (400°F/Gas Mark 6) for about 40 minutes.

Remove from the oven and allow to cool in the tin before turning out.

Potato Bread

500 g (18 oz) floury potatoes
40 g (1 ½ oz) yeast
300 ml (½ pt) water
300 ml (½ pt) milk
1 kg (2 ¼ lb) semolina
2 tsp salt
nutmeg

Peel the potatoes and boil them in salted water for about 20 minutes. Drain in a colander and leave to cool a little, then mash until smooth.

Dissolve the yeast in 6 tablespoons of mixed lukewarm water and milk.

Sift the semolina and salt into a bowl, add the nutmeg, then knead the potatoes with the semolina to make a smooth dough. Add the dissolved yeast and the remaining liquid to the dough and knead thoroughly.

Cover the dough and leave to prove in a warm place for about 2 hours, until it has doubled in volume.

Knead again thoroughly and, with floured hands, shape the dough into a round loaf. Stand the loaf on a floured baking sheet, cover with a damp cloth and leave to prove for a further 30 minutes.

Bake in the oven at 220°C (425°F/Gas Mark 7) for about 45 minutes, until crusty and golden brown.

Potato Brioche

750 g (1 ⅔ lb) floury potatoes

2 eggs

2 tsp salt

cayenne pepper

nutmeg

butter for greasing

1 finger-thick slice Emmenthal cheese

60 g (2 oz) butter, melted

breadcrumbs

Peel the potatoes and boil in salted water for about 20 minutes. Drain, then mash until smooth.

Place in the oven at minimum setting for about 12 minutes to dry out. Stir the eggs into the mashed potatoes to make a dough, and season with salt, cayenne pepper and nutmeg.

Divide the dough into two-thirds and one-third of the quantity. Shape the larger quantity into 10 balls to fit in a ramekin dish, and the smaller quantity into 10 smaller balls.

Butter 10 ramekins and place one large ball in each. Using a knife, make a groove about 1 cm (½ in) deep across each ball.

Cut the cheese into 10 equal-sized cubes and insert 1 cube into each groove. Place a small ball on top of each brioche and brush with melted butter. Sprinkle with breadcrumbs and bake in the oven at 200°C (400°F/Gas Mark 6) for 15–20 minutes until the brioches are golden brown and crusty

Potato Sticks

150 g (5 oz) floury potatoes

150 g (5 oz) butter

150 g (5 oz) plain flour

salt

1 egg yolk

2 tbsp single cream

coarse salt

poppy seeds

caraway seeds

Peel the potatoes and boil in salted water for about 20 minutes. Drain in a colander and allow to cool.

Coarsely grate the potatoes. Mix the grated potatoes with butter and flour, and season with salt.

Knead to a smooth dough, divide into 4 portions and shape each portion into a roll. Cut each roll into 16 pieces.

Roll each piece into a 'finger' and, using a knife, make several incisions across each one.

Beat the egg and cream together, and brush each finger with the mixture.

Sprinkle one-third of the sticks with salt, one-third with poppy seeds and the rest with caraway seeds. Bake in the oven at 200°C (400°F/Gas Mark 6) for 10–12 minutes until golden.

Potato Croissants

500 g (18 oz) floury potatoes

salt

freshly ground pepper

20 black olives, stoned

1 tbsp oil

1 onion, finely chopped

100 g (3 ½ oz) ewe's milk cheese, crumbled

1 bunch parsley, finely chopped

2 packets frozen puff pastry

flour for rolling

1 egg yolk

2 tbsp single cream

1 tbsp coarse salt

Peel the potatoes and boil for about 20 minutes in salted water.

Drain in a colander, leave to cool a little, then mash until smooth and season with salt and pepper.

Coarsely chop the olives.

Heat the oil in a small frying-pan and sauté the onion.

Stir the olives, cheese, onions and parsley into the potatoes.

On a floured work surface, roll out the pastry dough and cut into rectangles 18 x 10 cm (7 x 4 in). Cut each piece into 2 triangles.

Place 1 tablespoon of filling on each triangle, then roll from the base to the point.

Beat the egg and cream together. Brush the croissants with the mixture, then sprinkle with salt.

Bake in the oven at 200°C (400°F/Gas Mark 6) for 15–20 minutes until golden.

Serves 4
507 calories per serving

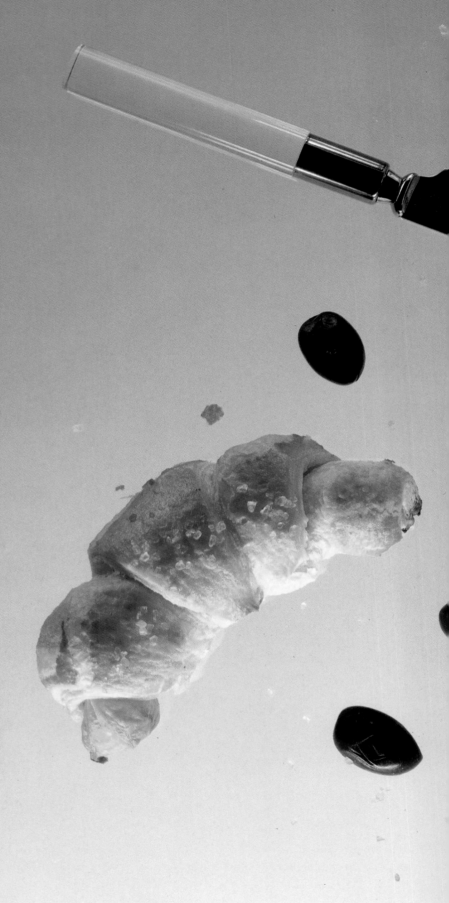

Potato Strudel

300 g (10 oz) sifted plain flour

1 egg

1 tsp salt

1 tsp oil

100 ml (3 ½ fl oz) warm water

½ tbsp vinegar

250 g (9 oz) floury potatoes

75 g (3 oz) butter

60 g (2 oz) sugar

2 egg yolks

juice and grated rind of 1 lemon

50 g (2 oz) finely ground almonds

115 ml (4 fl oz) single cream

50 g (2 oz) sultanas

2 egg whites, stiffly beaten

breadcrumbs

icing sugar for dusting

Make a well in the middle of the sifted flour and add the egg, salt and oil. Mix the water and vinegar and add a little at a time to the flour, then quickly knead to a smooth dough. Leave to stand for about 15 minutes.

Peel the potatoes and boil them in salted water for about 20 minutes. Drain and mash until smooth while still hot.

Beat 60 g (2 oz) of butter until it becomes fluffy, and gradually stir in the sugar. Add the egg yolks and stir until creamy. Stir in the lemon rind and juice, almonds, cream and sultanas, then add to the dough and mix thoroughly. Fold in the egg whites.

Roll out the dough on a large floured cloth, then pull it into a thin sheet 50 x 70 cm (20 x 28 in). Sprinkle on the breadcrumbs, leaving a border of 3 cm (1 ⅛ in) all round, and spread the filling on top. Starting at one of the long sides, roll the pastry up and firmly seal the edges.

Grease a baking sheet with about 15 g (½ oz) butter and place the strudel on it. Melt the remaining butter and brush it over the strudel. Bake in the oven at 220°C (425°F/Gas Mark 7) for about 50 minutes until golden brown. Dust with icing sugar.

Serves 4
777 calories per serving

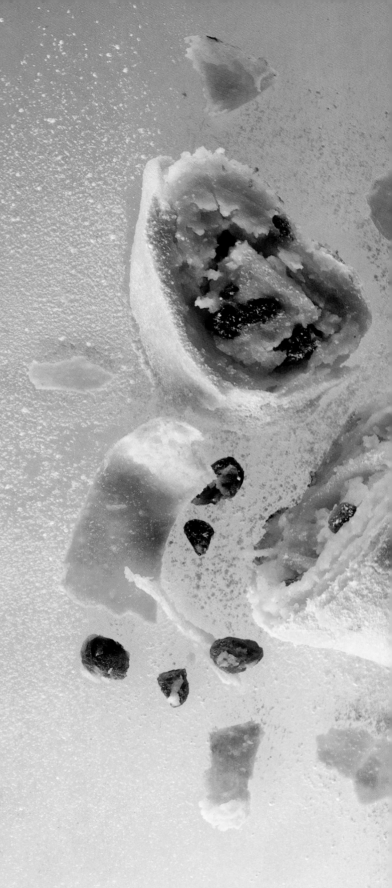

Almond Cake

400 g (14 oz) floury potatoes, boiled in their skins
180 g (6 ¼ oz) sugar
8 eggs, separated
100 g (3 ½ oz) almonds, finely chopped
100 g (3 ½ oz) ground almonds
pinch each of salt, ground cloves and ground cardamom
grated rind of 1 lemon
pulp from ½ vanilla pod
butter for greasing
breadcrumbs to line the mould
225 g (8 oz) plain chocolate
Optional: icing sugar for dusting

Cook the potatoes a day in advance. When you are ready to bake, peel and grate them.

Whisk the sugar and egg yolks until frothy, then fold in the grated potatoes.

Add the chopped and ground almonds, salt and spices, lemon rind and vanilla pulp, and stir thoroughly.

Beat the egg whites until stiff, then carefully fold into the mixture.

Grease a fluted cake mould about 25 cm (10 in) in diameter with butter and sprinkle with breadcrumbs.

Pour the dough into the mould and bake in the oven at 200°C (400°F/Gas Mark 6) for about 60 minutes. **Do not** open the oven door during the baking time.

Turn off the heat and leave the cake to stand in the oven for a further 20 minutes.

Remove the cake from the oven and turn out onto a wire cooling rack.

Melt the chocolate and pour over the cake.

If you like, sprinkle with icing sugar.

The cake will be very dark in colour, but this does not spoil the flavour.

Serves 4
879 calories per serving

Side Salads

You don't have to be an artist to turn a salad into a work of art. Nature has designed salad leaves, vegetables and herbs in such a way that they create their own beautiful designs, so we urge you to serve salads on a flat plate rather than in a bowl. This also has advantages both for flavour and fragrance. Sprinkled sparingly over the salad, dressings combine with the ingredients without swamping them.

You can, of course, serve a salad with any potato dish. With many recipes in this book, we have suggested the salads that harmonize best with specific dishes.

1
Rocket with Quail Eggs

250 g (9 oz) rocket

8 quail eggs

100 g (3 ½ oz) sliced smoked bacon

4 slices white bread, crusts removed

2 tbsp oil

1 small packet cress

3 tbsp red wine vinegar

9 tbsp olive oil

salt

freshly ground pepper

Sort the rocket. Wash and drain thoroughly.

Place the quail eggs in boiling water and cook for 4 minutes, rinse under cold running water, then shell and halve.

Fry or grill the bacon until crisp.

Finely dice the bread. Heat the oil in a frying-pan and fry the bread until golden brown.

Chop the cress with kitchen scissors.

For the dressing, combine the vinegar, olive oil, salt and pepper.

Toss the rocket in the dressing and arrange on individual plates. Arrange the quail eggs, bacon and croûtons on top, sprinkle with cress, and drizzle the rest of the dressing on top.

2
French Bean and Pear Salads

450 g (1 lb) french beans

15 g (½ oz) butter

100 g (3 ½ oz) pine-nuts

2 William pears

20 red grapes

leaves of 1 bunch mint

3 tbsp cider vinegar

9 tbsp pistachio oil

salt

freshly ground pepper

Top and tail the beans, then cut diagonally into pieces. Place in boiling salted water and cook for 4 minutes. Drain in a colander and rinse under cold running water.

Heat the butter in a frying-pan and fry the pine-nuts until golden.

Thinly slice the pears and grapes lengthways. Cut half the mint into thin strips.

To make the dressing, mix vinegar, oil, salt and pepper, and stir in the strips of mint.

Arrange the beans, pears and grapes on individual plates, and sprinkle with pine nuts. Drizzle the dressing over the salad, and garnish with whole mint leaves.

3
Oak-Leaf Lettuce with Diced Vegetables

1 oak-leaf lettuce
2 carrots, diced
1 leek, light green parts only, diced
½ stick celery, diced
1 tomato, peeled, deseeded and diced
7 tbsp oil
1 onion, finely chopped
100 g (3 ½ oz) mung-bean sprouts
1 tbsp mustard
3 tbsp red wine vinegar
salt
freshly ground pepper
sugar

Sort, wash and thoroughly dry the lettuce.

Cook the carrots, leek and celery in boiling water, or steam, until tender but still crisp. Drain in a colander, then rinse under cold running water.

Heat 1 tablespoon of oil in a frying-pan and sauté the onion until transparent.

Mix the onion with mustard, vinegar, the remaining oil, salt, pepper and sugar, then beat in a blender until frothy.

Toss the lettuce in the dressing and arrange on individual plates. Sprinkle with vegetables and bean sprouts, and drizzle the remaining dressing on top.

4
Grapefruit, Pomegranate and Radish Salad

1 green lettuce	
1 lollo rosso	
1 curly endive	
1 small radicchio	
1 pink grapefruit	
1 pomegranate	
1 bunch radishes	
leaves from small bunch parsley	
3 tbsp vinegar	
9 tbsp oil	
salt	
freshly ground pepper	
sugar	

Sort, wash and thoroughly dry the salad leaves.

Peel the grapefruit, remove the pith and cut into wedges.

Remove the seeds from the pomegranate.

Slice the radishes.

Mix the vinegar, oil, salt, pepper and sugar for the dressing.

Toss the salad leaves in the dressing and arrange on individual plates.

Arrange the grapefruit, pomegranate seeds, radishes and parsley on top, then sprinkle with the rest of the dressing.

5
Tomato Salad

4 beef tomatoes

2 shallots

1 bunch basil

3 tbsp balsamic vinegar

9 tbsp olive oil

salt

freshly ground pepper

Wash the tomatoes, remove the stalks and the hard flesh surrounding them, then slice lengthways.

Peel the shallots and cut crossways into thin slices.

Tear off the basil leaves.

To make the dressing, mix the vinegar, oil, salt and pepper.

Arrange the tomatoes and shallots on individual plates, and drizzle the dressing on top. Serve sprinkled with basil.

6
Chicory and Beetroot Salad

4 chicory bulbs

2 beetroot

1 bunch chives

3 tbsp lemon juice

9 tbsp peanut oil

50 g (2 oz) capers

salt

freshly ground pepper

Separate the chicory, discarding the bitter stalk. Wash and leave to drain.

Cook the beetroot in boiling salted water for 20 minutes. Drain in a colander and leave to cool.

Peel the beetroot and cut into thin strips.

Wash the chives and cut diagonally into long strips.

To make the dressing, mix the lemon juice, oil, salt and pepper, then stir in the capers.

Arrange the chicory and beetroot on individual plates and drizzle the dressing on top. Serve sprinkled with chives.

7
Green Asparagus and Walnut Salad

1 kg (2 ¼ lb) green asparagus, woody ends removed

100 g (3 ½ oz) shelled walnuts, chopped

1 bunch watercress

3 tbsp raspberry vinegar

9 tbsp walnut oil

salt

freshly ground pepper

Cook the asparagus in boiling salted water, or steam, until tender but still crisp. Drain in a colander, briefly rinse under cold water, then drain again.

Wash the watercress and tear off the leaves. Cut half the leaves into thin strips.

To make the dressing, mix the vinegar, oil, salt and pepper, then stir in the chopped watercress.

Arrange the asparagus and walnuts on individual plates, and drizzle the dressing on top. Serve sprinkled with watercress leaves.

178

8
Avocado Salad with Caviare Cream Dressing

2 ripe avocados
lemon juice
10 cherry tomatoes
1 bunch tarragon
200 g (7 oz) crème fraîche
50 ml (2 fl oz) single cream
50 g (2 oz) salmon caviare
salt
freshly ground pepper

Peel and halve the avocados, removing the stones. Slice the avocados crossways, and sprinkle with lemon juice. Slice the cherry tomatoes crossways.

Finely chop 1–2 stalks of tarragon. Tear off the leaves from the rest of the bunch.

To make the dressing, mix the crème fraîche, cream, salt, pepper and chopped tarragon.

Pour the dressing onto individual plates. Arrange the avocados and tomatoes on top, and serve sprinkled with caviare and tarragon leaves.

Vinegar and Oil

It is the dressing that turns a few green leaves into an exquisite salad. And it is vinegar and oil that make the dressing. There is such a wide range of both that you could create a new and exciting dressing every day. Vinegar and oil should be combined to make the best of their individual flavours. Pungent vinegars, like raspberry and sherry, should be used with subtly flavoured oil. Similarly, strong-tasting oils, such as hazelnut or walnut, combine best with neutral-flavoured vinegar. Some of the vinegars and oils described on the following pages are widely available; others might be found in delicatessens and speciality food shops.

Potato vinegar

Vinegar essence

Fruit vinegar Herb vinegar

Balsamic vinegar

Sherry vinegar

Raspberry vinegar

Vinegar brings out the flavour of herbs and spices, but only when used sparingly so that the acidity is not overwhelming. Since some varieties are more acidic than others, getting the right mix is a matter of trial and error. Vinegar makes raw food more digestible because it stimulates the digestive juices, so vinegar is healthy too.

182

Pumpkin-seed oil

Hazelnut oil

Sesame oil

Walnut oil

Grapeseed oil

Olive oil

Pistachio oil

Oil makes salad leaves smoother and helps the dressing to cling to them. If you really enjoy the taste of oil, always choose the cold-pressed sort. Hot-pressed oils, or those extracted by chemical means and refined, lose their distinctive flavour and, unfortunately, some of their health-giving properties.

Glossary

Balsamic vinegar
Dark brown, mild, sweet and fragrant – for many people, this is the finest of all vinegars. An Italian speciality, it is made from grape must. The longer it is left to mature, the thicker it becomes. The most famous balsamic vinegars, some up to 20 years old, come from Modena. Some of them are even sold as 'vintage' vinegars.

Champagne vinegar
Produced from champagne, the aroma of this vinegar is more delicate than that of white-wine vinegar, but the flavour is similar.

Cider vinegar
Mild and fruity, this familiar vinegar is produced from apple must or from ripe apples.

Herb vinegars
These vinegars are based on wine or spirit vinegar, to which various kinds of aromatic herbs are added. The best kinds are made from pure wine vinegar with a single fresh herb, not herb extract.

Malt vinegar
A sharp vinegar with a high acid content, it is used mainly on fish and chips, not on salads.

Potato vinegar
Mildly acid, with a subtle potato flavour, this German speciality is made from potato spirit to which newly pressed potato juice has been added.

Raspberry vinegar
Wine vinegar matured with fresh raspberries has a delicate raspberry smell and flavour.

Sherry vinegar
Resembling sherry both in smell and subtle flavour, this vinegar is made from a blend of wine and sherry.

Wine vinegar
The best kinds of wine vinegar have a strong wine flavour. In some of them you can even detect the grape variety. The colour depends on whether red or white wine has been used.

Grapeseed oil
This is a dark green oil, extracted from dried seeds of wine grapes, and has an almost neutral taste. Since it contains a high proportion of unsaturated fatty acids, it is regarded as particularly healthy.

Hazelnut oil
Cold-pressed from hazelnuts, this oil has a strong, very nutty flavour. It turns rancid after only a few months, so should be bought only in small quantities.

Herb oil

The flavour varies according to which herbs have been added: tarragon, basil, rosemary, thyme or a mixture of Provençal herbs. It also depends on the quality of the oil. Cold-pressed, neutral-tasting oil is used to produce the best herb oils.

Linseed oil

Produced from the seed of the flax plant, also known as linseed, this oil has a strong and very distinctive nutty flavour, but does not keep for long.

Olive oil

Olives can vary in flavour from very mild to powerful. The colours range from pale yellow to dark green, but this is no indicator of quality. The best olive oil, called 'first pressing' and designated by the EC as 'extra virgin olive oil' is cold-pressed from fresh olives. Italy, Spain, France and Greece all produce cold-pressed oil, but the finest of all comes from the oil mills of Tuscany and Liguria.

Peanut oil

If it is cold-pressed, the oil has a strong peanut flavour. Usually, however, it is extracted and refined, and the flavour is somewhat neutral with only a hint of peanuts.

Pumpkin-seed oil

This oil has an intense, exquisitely nutty flavour and is very dark green in colour (the darker the colour, the better the quality). It is cold-pressed from the seeds of a special kind of pumpkin and is not widely available.

Salad and cooking oil

Pale vegetable oils with a completely neutral taste are hot-pressed or extracted from a variety of oils, including peanut, corn, sunflower and soya oils. To give them better keeping qualities, they are chemically purified (refined). They are not recommended for salads.

Sesame oil

The sesame seeds are roasted before being cold-pressed. The oil has a pleasant, nutty taste. Dark sesame oil has a stronger flavour than the lighter sort.

Walnut oil

With its mild and distinctly nutty taste, this is an aristocrat among oils, especially suited for refined salads. Once opened, it will keep for only a few months.

A large proportion of the potatoes we eat are processed. For people who shop only occasionally or have limited time in which to prepare meals, products such as canned or bottled peeled potatoes, potato salad and instant mashed potato are invaluable.

There is, of course, also a vast range of potato snacks. In addition to potato hoops, twirls and sticks, there is the crisp, which is made in a seemingly endless variety of flavours and shapes.

Processed Potato Products

*Frozen
Potato
Products*

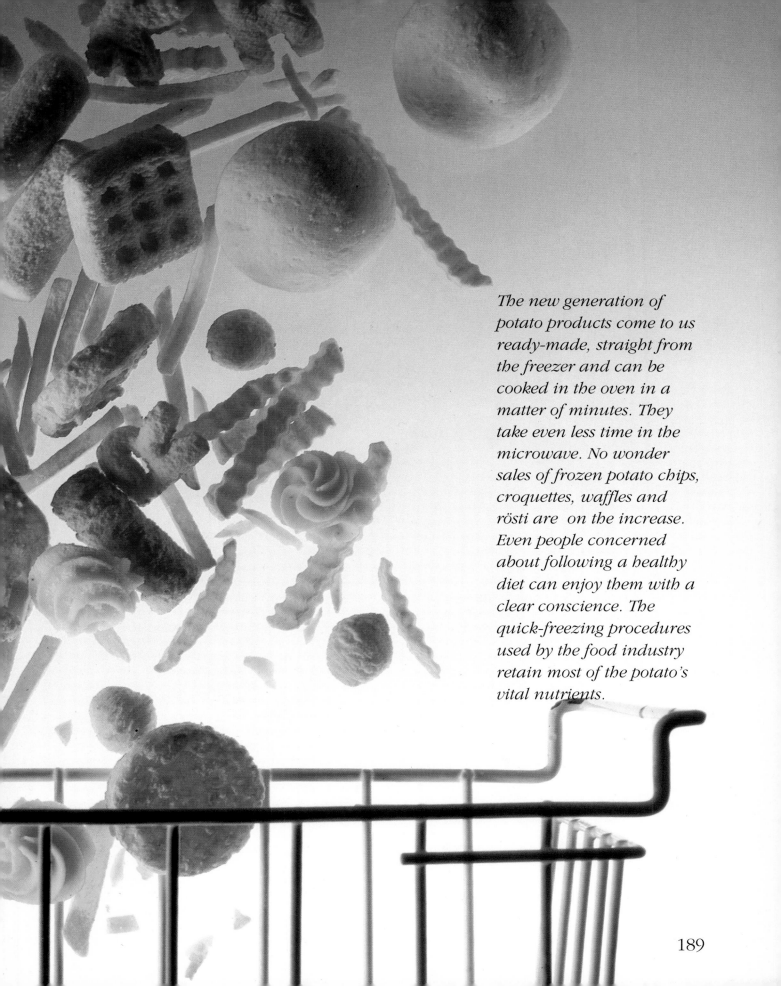

The new generation of potato products come to us ready-made, straight from the freezer and can be cooked in the oven in a matter of minutes. They take even less time in the microwave. No wonder sales of frozen potato chips, croquettes, waffles and rösti are on the increase. Even people concerned about following a healthy diet can enjoy them with a clear conscience. The quick-freezing procedures used by the food industry retain most of the potato's vital nutrients.